Published By
Gaslight Publishing Pty. Ltd.
3/397 Riley St., Surry Hills, NSW 2010 Australia
Telephone (02) 212 2522 Facsimile (02) 212 6428

© Gaslight Publishing Pty. Ltd. 1988

Manuscripts	Lynette G. Roach	Chapter Introductions	Marilyn Abel
Project Home Economist and Food Editor	Ellen Argyriou	Designed By	Yon Tarpstra
Food Photography	Gary Isaacs	Graphic Art and Typesetting	Gas Graphics TGC Pty. Ltd. Sydney, Australia
	John Bolton		
	Peter Macintosh	Original Concept	Lynette G. Roach
	Peter Thompson		
	Phil Wymant	Recipe Development	The Recipe Development Centre Sydney, Australia
Home Economist and Food Stylists	Margaret Hill		
	Jan Hamilton	Printer	Griffin Press
	Carol Reilly		Netley, South Australia
			First Printing
Location Photography	Hugh Scarlett		March 1988

Additional Photography provided by: Bread Research Institute of Australia,
Australian Picture Library, Wildlight Photo Agency, Allan Hedges, Horizon International,
Ozsport/Leon Faivre, Northern Territory Tourist Commission, Tourism Australia, and the Tourist
Commissions of; New South Wales, Victoria, Queensland, South Australia, Tasmania and Western Australia.

National Library of Australia Cataloguing-In-Publication Data
The Australian Heritage Cookbook
Includes Index
ISBN   0   7316   0728   7
1. Cookery 2. Cookery – Australia – History
641.5

Photographs Preceeding Pages

Pages 2/3
Harbour by Night, Circular Quay
Sydney, New South Wales

Page 4/5
View Over Middle Harbour
Sydney, New South Wales

Photographs Following Pages

Pages 8/9
At Dusk
Launceston, Tasmania

Pages 10
Bourke Street
Melbourne, Victoria

Pages 12/13
Hainault Goldmine
Kalgoorlie, Western Australia

CONTENTS

INTRODUCTION

Australians are fortunate in so many ways – indeed, to be a cook in this wonderful country is both a privilege and a pleasure. The abundance of natural good food makes the Australian food industry one of the most self sufficient in the world. There are plentiful supplies of meat, grains, fruit and vegetables, dairy produce and seafood available throughout the year. Furthermore, there is an excellent wine industry which produces world class quality wines and liqueurs.

This beautifully illustrated cookery book caters for every occasion – from spontaneous entertaining and family cooking to more extravagant recipes for that special dinner party. Australians love to entertain and our marvellous climate lends itself perfectly to both unsophisticated and formal entertaining.

Australian country cooking is delightful and the section devoted to this contains many old-fashioned recipes brought by our early settlers. There has been a growing enthusiasm for all types of natural cooking and the results of home pickling, preserving and bread making are invariably tastier and cheaper than shop-bought varieties.

For Australians on the move, there is a special section full of tempting recipes for microwave cooking. Anything which is time saving and economical is naturally desirable and microwave cooking can produce the simplest of meals as well as an exotic banquet with the minimum of fuss. Simply wonderful for the busy Australian.

The Australian meat industry offers an excellent quality and variety of beef, veal, lamb, pork and poultry. We can prepare traditional roasts and also obtain the best value from less expensive cuts of meats by using aromatic herbs and creamy sauces. Barbeques are always delicious and are a most popular and casual way of serving meat, keeping the nutrients intact while remaining tender and juicy.

The chapter on fish and shellfish will inspire the cook to make full use of the enormous range of seafood available from our surrounding waters. Exotic fish and succulent crayfish, oysters, prawns and crab lend themselves naturally to delightful recipes which will satisfy everyone's taste.

With 45% of Australia in the tropics, it is only natural that a section be devoted to tropical cooking. There is a host of succulent fruit – pineapples, mangoes, paw paws, rockmelon, avocadoes and passionfruit. Served alone or in conjunction with our beautiful seafood, they provide the ingredients for cool, mouth-watering recipes.

The enormous influence of our multi-national population is evident in our cosmopolitan diet. International recipes offer all Australians the opportunity to experiment and broaden their repertoire of recipes to include exotic foreign delicacies. Every imaginable ingredient is available.

The Australian Heritage Cookbook, deserves a place in every kitchen. Full of delicious, nutritious recipes for every occasion, it will provide satisfaction and challenge for every cook. May this book give enthusiasm, creativity and pleasure to the essential art of cooking.

BOUNTY FROM OCEANS RIVERS AND STREAMS

With over 2,500 species of fish surrounding our island continent, Australia has an astonishing variety of fish, as well as shellfish, to choose from. With such variety, the choice is more than ample to satisfy everyone's taste and is a perpetual delight to both the cook and diner.

Fish shops which once stocked old favourites such as flake and flathead, now stock a wide and exciting range of fish to tempt us. Gemfish, jewfish, redfish, flounder, sole and John Dory — to name a few. Fresh shellfish are unbeatable for flavour and are very nutritious.

It is extremely important to know, not only how to cook fresh fish but how to buy them.

Always buy on the day the fish is to be used. Check they have full bright eyes, gills which are flat and red underneath, feel slippery to touch and most of all have a "sea smell".

Any traveller to Australia should not go home without sampling the rock lobster from Western Australia, crayfish from Tasmania, oysters from Sydney, delicious Northern Territory barramundi, and the giant Queensland mud crabs.

This section will inspire the cook to make full use of the enormous range of seafood available from our surrounding waters — enough to tempt anyone who loves seafood.

Photograph page 14:
Unloading the catch

Whiting Rolls or Whiting Paupiettes

(Photograph page 16)

The delicate flavouring of the whiting enhances the flavour of the prawns.

250g (8oz) green prawns, shelled
¼ cup chopped shallots
220g (7oz) butter or margarine
1.5kg (3lb) whiting fillets
1 onion, chopped
water and milk
seasoning to taste
cornflour for thickening

Blend the prawns, shallots, butter, seasoning in a food processor until smooth. Spread a little of the prawn paste onto each fillet, roll up and secure with a toothpick. Place with the onions in a baking dish with sufficient water and milk to cover. Bake, covered, at 180°C (350°F) until the fish paste is cooked. Remove and keep warm. Combine the cornflour with the stock, bring to the boil and stir until the mixture thickens. Serve the sauce poured over the fish rolls garnished with lemon and sprigs of dill.
Serves 6.

Cheese-Topped Gemfish on Mushrooms

4 tablespoons butter or margarine
1 cup mushrooms, sliced
750g (1½lb) smoked gemfish
⅓ cup dry white wine
2 bay leaves
⅓ cup cream
½ cup grated cheese
½ cup fresh breadcrumbs
sliced tomato for garnishing
Seasoning to taste.

Melt the butter in a frying pan, add the mushrooms and sauté for 1 minute. Remove from the pan and scatter over the base of a greased casserole dish. Place the fish on top, pour over the wine and add the bay leaves. Cover and cook at 180°C (350°F) for 10 minutes. Remove the bay leaf and add the cream and season. Sprinkle with the cheese and breadcrumbs. Return to the oven for 10 minutes. Serve garnished with tomato slices.
Serves 4.

Photograph opposite:
Peaches and Squid (Recipe this page)

Photograph opposite page:
Whiting Rolls (Recipe this page)

Peaches and Squid

(Photograph this page)

The flesh of squid is delicious and succulent, and although a little fiddly to prepare, its worth the wait. If you don't have the time, commercially prepared squid is available from your local supermarket.

60g (2oz) butter or margarine
½ cup chopped onion
750g (1½lb) squid tubes, rings or slices
1 cup sliced peaches
¼ cup orange liqueur
chopped chives
Seasoning to taste.

Melt the butter in a frying pan and add the onion. Sauté until tender then stir in the squid and gently cook until it changes in colour. Stir in the peaches, liqueur and seasoning. Cook for a further 3 minutes and serve with cooked pasta garnished with chopped chives.
Serves 6.

Scallops in Sour Cream with Mushrooms

Do not overcook the scallops as they will toughen. These are delicious served on a bed of saffron rice accompanied with a fresh herb and cucumber salad.

1½ tablespoons butter or margarine
2 cups mushrooms, roughly chopped
¼ cup shallots, chopped
750g (1½lb) scallops
1 cup sour cream
½ teaspoon curry powder
2 teaspoons lemon juice
cornflour to thicken
Seasoning to taste.

Melt the butter in a saucepan and add the mushrooms and shallots and sauté 2-3 minutes. Season and add the scallops, sour cream, curry powder and lemon juice. Cook for a further 2 minutes and thicken with cornflour if wished.
Serves 4.

Crumbed Scallops on Peach and Carrot Puree

1 x 425g (14oz) can* peaches may replace fresh peaches when not in season. These should be well drained then pureed with the cooked carrots.

1 cup breadcrumbs
½ teaspoon salt
½ cup apricot brandy
36 scallops
220g (7oz) butter or margarine, melted

The Puree:

2 carrots
2 peaches, peeled, sliced
⅓ cup cream
2 tablespoons apricot brandy
*nearest equivalent can size.

Combine the breadcrumbs with the salt into a mixing bowl and stir in approximately ¼ cup apricot brandy. Dip the scallops into the butter and coat with the breadcrumbs and refrigerate for 1 hour. Steam the carrots and peaches until soft then puree in a blender or food processor with the cream and the apricot brandy. Keep warm. Pan fry the crumbed scallops until just browned, being careful not to overcook them. Serve on a base of the puree, garnished with fresh herbs.
Serves 6.

Cheesy Grilled Redfish with Sour Cream Sauce

(Photograph this page)

1 lettuce
1 bunch silverbeet
4 shallots chopped
6 slices Gouda cheese
6 slices smoked salmon
12 redfish fillets
1 tablespoon capers chopped
½ teaspoon salt
1 cup sour cream

Finely shred the lettuce and silverbeet and lightly steam and cool. Puree in a food processor together with the shallots and reheat. Sandwich the slices of cheese and smoked salmon between two fillets of fish, secure with toothpicks and grill until cooked and cheese has melted. Combine the capers, salt and sour cream. Serve the sandwiches of fish with the vegetable puree and the sour cream sauce.
Serves 6.

Crayfish and Scallop Supreme

A delightful fish combination of these two popular Australian fish.

2 cups rice
1kg (2lb) crayfish
3 tablespoons butter or margarine
2 tablespoons lemon juice
750g (1½lb) scallops
6 shallots, chopped
1 tablespoon chopped parsley

Cook rice in boiling salted water for 12-15 minutes. Drain and keep warm. Halve the crayfish lengthwise and remove the digestive tract. Chop flesh into bite size pieces. Melt 1 tablespoon of the butter in a frying pan with the lemon juice and sauté scallops and shallots until just tender. Add the crayfish and allow to heat through. Toss parsley and remaining butter through rice and spoon onto a heated serving plate. Spoon the seafood mixture into the shells and serve with the rice.
Serves 4.

Photograph above:
Cheesy Grilled Redfish with Sour Cream Sauce
(Recipe this page)

Prawns in a Coffee Cream Sauce

Prawns cooked in this way could be chopped and used as a filling for vol-au-vents.

30g (1oz) butter or margarine
30 large green prawns, shelled, deveined
2 tablespoons brandy
¼ cup coffee cream liqueur
¼ cup cream
½ teaspoon salt
1 tablespoon desiccated coconut

Melt the butter in a frying pan and stir fry the prawns until just cooked. Pour in the brandy and flambé, add the coffee cream liqueur, cream and salt and stir over a low heat until the sauce thickens. Serve the prawns with cooked pasta and sprinkle with desiccated coconut.
Serves 6.

Crusty-Topped Redfish Loaf

1 tablespoon butter or margarine
1 tablespoon flour
1 cup milk
500g (1lb) redfish fillets, poached, flaked
2 cups fresh breadcrumbs
1 onion, finely chopped
1 capsicum, finely chopped
½ cup chopped bacon
½ cup grated Cheddar cheese
extra breadcrumbs for topping
1 tablespoon butter or margarine
Seasoning to taste.

Make a sauce in the usual way with the butter, flour and milk. Season to taste then combine with the redfish, breadcrumbs, onion and capsicum. Grease and line a loaf tin and alternate the fish mixture with the bacon and cheese ending with a layer of fish. Sprinkle with extra breadcrumbs and dot with butter. Bake at 190°C (370°F) for approximately 1 hour.
Serves 6-8.

Crayfish and Sprout Salad

A delicious recipe.

1½ cups Pernod
4 large sorrel leaves, finely shredded
¼ cup finely chopped celery
¼ teaspoon chilli sauce
500g (1lb) cooked crayfish
alfalfa sprouts

Combine the mayonnaise, Pernod sorrel, celery and chilli sauce. Chop the crayfish into bite-size pieces and gently fold into the sauce. Serve the crayfish on a bed of sprouts with thin slices of buttered wholemeal bread.
Serve 4 — 6.

The Crayfish is found in great quantities on the South Eastern and Western coasts of Tasmania. Southern Crayfish is also known as "Southern Rock Lobster". The annual catch is in the region of 1,500 tonnes.
Southern Rock Lobsters are recognised as a gourmet's delight and are exported both live and frozen to all parts of the world. The most popular size for the gourmet market is for lobster under 800g (approx 2lb).

Photograph opposite:
Crayfish Catch

Oysters au Fromage

Parmesan or Gruyére cheese could be used to add extra flavour to the oysters

2 rashers bacon, chopped
¼ cup chopped shallots
90g (3oz) grated tasty cheese
1 tablespoon Worcestershire sauce
12 oysters
3 lettuce leaves, shredded
Seasoning to taste.

Sauté the bacon and shallots in a frying pan for 2 minutes, drain. Combine the cheese, bacon mixture, Worcestershire sauce and seasoning in a bowl. Place the oysters on a baking sheet and top with a spoonful of cheese mixture. Grill until cheese has melted and browned. Serve on the lettuce, garnished with sprigs of parsley.
Serves 2.

Tahitian Fish and Macaroni Salad

220g (7oz) white fish
1 medium onion, peeled, sliced
juice 2 lemons
½ cup coconut milk
½ cup cream
1 tablespoon whisky
dash of Tabasco sauce
½ teaspoon chopped fresh parsley
3 cups cooked macaroni

Cut the fish fillets into very thin slices across the grain and place in a glass dish with the onion, lemon juice, coconut milk, cream, whisky, Tabasco and parsley. Marinate for at least 24 hours in the refrigerator. Combine the macaroni with the fish and spoon into lettuce cups just prior to serving.
Serves 6.

Rolled Fillets with Health Filling

3 slices wholemeal bread, crumbed
½ cup sultanas
¼ cup walnuts
1 tablespoon lemon juice
little orange juice to bind
500g (1lb) fish fillets, redfish, bream
wheatgerm for coating
oil for deep fat frying

Puree the wholemeal crumbs, sultanas and walnuts in a blender or food processor.
Add the juices and continue processing until a soft mixture is achieved.
Spread a layer of the filling onto each fillet, then roll up and secure. Coat the fillets with wheatgerm and deep fry in oil until golden.
Serve with sauteed silverbeet and a carrot and apple salad.
Serves 4.

Fillets of Fish Provencale

1kg (2lb) sea bream fillets, skinned
nutmeg
1 tablespoon olive oil
1 large onion, sliced
1 red capsicum, seeded, sliced
56g (1-2oz) can* anchovy fillets, drained
1 tomato, sliced
1 tablespoon stuffed olives
½ cup sliced mushrooms
½ cup white wine
15g (½oz) butter or margarine
Seasoning to taste.
*nearest equivalent can size.

Sprinkle fish fillets with seasoning and nutmeg, pour the olive oil into an ovenproof dish with the onion and capsicum and arrange the fish on top. Scatter with the remaining ingredients and dot with butter.
Cover and bake at 180°C (350°F) for 40 minutes or until cooked.
Serves 4.

Grilled Marinated Scallops

Bacon adds a marvellous flavour to all fish.

1 tablespoon lemon juice
1 clove crushed garlic
1 teaspoon finely chopped fennel
3 tablespoons peanut oil
2 teaspoons soy sauce
½ teaspoon crushed green peppercorns
500g (1lb) scallops
250g (8oz) bacon rashers, rind removed

Combine the first seven ingredients in a bowl to make a marinade. Wash and clean the scallops, stir into the marinade and leave for 1½ hours. Drain and wrap each scallop in a piece of bacon. Thread onto skewers and grill for 5-7 minutes. The bacon should be crisp so turn the scallops once or twice during the cooking being careful not to overcook.
Serves 4-6.

Photograph above:
Processing Prawns — Darwin, Northern Territory

Smoked Cod Casserole

(Photograph page 21)

Haddock could be used in this recipe, in place of the smoked cod.

1kg (2lb) smoked cod
1 onion, sliced
1 cup dry white wine
peppercorns
1 small clove garlic, crushed
little chopped fennel or dill
4 tomatoes, quartered
few black olives
6 shallots sliced

Cut fish into serving pieces and place in a casserole with the onion, wine, peppercorns, garlic and herbs. Cover and bake at 180°C (350°F) for 30-40 minutes adding the tomatoes and olives during the last ½ hour of cooking. Serve the fish with its juice, garnished with shallots.
Serves 6-8.

Photograph opposite:
Smoked Cod Casserole.

Sea Scallops in a Honey and Dill Mayonnaise

The honey in the mayonnaise provides an interesting flavour to the fish.

1kg (2lb) scallops
fish stock
The Mayonnaise:
3 egg yolks
1 teaspoon vinegar
1½ cups vegetable oil
2 tablespoons honey
2 tablespoons chopped dill
Seasoning to taste

Poach the scallops in the stock until just cooked. Drain, cool and refrigerate. Make a mayonnaise in the food processor by combining the egg yolks with the vinegar and slowly dribbling in the oil. Transfer to a bowl and add honey, dill and seasoning. Stir the scallops into the mayonnaise and serve in a scallop shell on a bed of watercress.
Serves 6.

Baked Seafood Avocado

2 avocados
1 cup crab meat
½ cup white sauce
¼ cup brown breadcrumbs
¼ cup grated cheese

Halve the avocados removing the seed. Mould a little crab into the cavity, spoon over some white sauce and top with the combined breadcrumbs and cheese. Bake at 220°C (440°F) until the cheese has melted. Serve at once as an entree.
Serves 4.

Fruit topped Ling Fillets

500g (1lb) ling fillets
1 onion, finely sliced
1 orange, peeled, finely sliced
2 bananas, peeled, finely sliced
2 tablespoons lemon juice
lemon pepper
salt to taste

Place the ling fillets on a sheet of lightly buttered foil, layer with the onion, orange and bananas. Pour over the lemon juice. Season with the lemon pepper, and salt.
Fold the foil over to form a neat parcel, and seal well. Cook on the barbecue for approximately 10-12 minutes. The fish is cooked when it flakes easily with a fork.
Serve with a spinach and cashew nut salad.
Serves 4.

Red Salmon Mousse

(Photograph this page)
This is an excellent dish for a buffet accompanied with salads and cold dishes.

Aspic Glaze:
2 tablespoons lemon juice
2 teaspoons gelatine
2 radishes thinly sliced
2 gherkins sliced into strips
1 olive
5 cup salmon mould
Seasoning to taste.

The Mousse:
1 x 250g (8oz) packet cream cheese, cubed
¾ cup yoghurt
½ cup mayonnaise
¼ cup gherkin juice
¼ cup lemon juice
5 teaspoons gelatine
2 x 220 (7oz) cans* red salmon, drained flaked
4 gherkins, sliced
10 stuffed olives, sliced
parsley and lemon wedges for garnish
*nearest equivalent can size

Heat the lemon juice with the seasoning in a saucepan, sprinkle over the gelatine, and stir until dissolved. Pour ¾ of mixture into the wetted salmon mould, and refrigerate until almost set, then arrange the radishes and gherkins in a decorative pattern using the olive for the eye, pour over the remaining aspic, refrigerate. Meanwhile combine the cheese, yoghurt and mayonnaise in a blender or food processor. Heat the juices in a small saucepan, sprinkle over the gelatine, and stir until dissolved. Add to the blended mixture with the salmon, gherkins and olives, blend until well combined. Pour the mixture onto the chilled aspic and refrigerate until firm. Unmould onto a serving platter and garnish with parsley and lemon wedges.
Serves 10 — 12.

Photograph above:
Red Salmon Mousse (Recipe this page)

Photograph opposite page:
Port Campbell, Victoria

Grilled Crayfish and Lemon-Annisette Butter

155g (5oz) butter
juice 1 lemon
2 tablespoons Pernod
1 teaspoon dill seeds or fennel
3 large green crayfish tails

Melt the butter in a saucepan and add the lemon juice, Pernod and dill. Stir well over medium heat and set to one side. Cut the crayfish tails in half removing the meat and cut into chunks and then return to the shell. Sit the tails on a grilling rack, brush liberally with the butter and place under the griller. Grill, brushing regularly with the butter until cooked. Serve with a tossed mixed lettuce and watercress salad. Serves 6.

Photograph following pages 26/27
Ocean Grange, 90 Mile Beach, Victoria

Photograph opposite page:
French Mussel Soup (Recipe this page)

Photograph below:
Trevally and Prawn Casserole (Recipe this page)

Grilled Creamy Crayfish

Always make sure the crayfish is very fresh when purchased, and cleaned thoroughly when halved.

3 medium,cooked crayfish
45g (1½oz) butter or margarine
1 small onion, chopped
4 tablespoons flour
1 cup milk
3 tablespoons cherry liqueur
2 tablespoons grated mild Cheddar cheese
2 teaspoons French mustard
½ teaspoon English mustard
breadcrumbs
butter

Halve the crayfish lengthwise and remove meat; cut into chunks. Melt the butter and sauté the onions until tender. Add the flour and stir over a low heat for 2 minutes. Gradually add the milk and allow the sauce to thicken. Add the liqueur and simmer for 2 minutes then stir in the cheese and mustards. Spoon a little of the sauce into the crayfish shells, add the crayfish and coat with the remaining sauce. Sprinkle with breadcrumbs and dot with butter. Grill until brown and bubbling. Serve immediately. Serves 6.

Trevally and Prawn Casserole

Photograph (this page)

If trevally is unavailable any white fish fillets would do.

1kg (2lb) trevally fillets
juice 1 lemon
water
2 cups white sauce
1 cup dry sherry
250g (8oz) cooked prawns, shelled, de-veined
2 firm tomatoes, sliced
1 green capsicum, seeded, sliced, blanched
Seasoning to taste.

Place fillets in a shallow dish, add the lemon juice and sufficient water to cover. Cover with foil and bake at 180°C (350°) for 10 minutes. Remove fish and cool. Reheat the white sauce and stir in the sherry and seasoning. Cut fish into pieces and stir into the sauce, together with the prawns, tomato and capsicum. Simmer until re-heated and serve hot, with a green salad. Serves 4.

French Mussel Soup

(Photograph page 25)

Although this is a soup recipe it is a meal in itself.

8 cups mussels
1 small onion, chopped
1 shallot, chopped
1 clove garlic, crushed
½ cup finely chopped parsley
freshly ground black pepper
75g (2½oz) butter or margarine
1¼ cups white wine
1½ tablespoons lemon juice

Scrub the mussels thoroughly and place in the saucepan with the onion, shallot, garlic, parsley, pepper, ½ the butter and the wine. Cover and cook the mussels for a few minutes over a high heat. Shake in the pan several times to ensure even cooking. When all the mussels have opened, transfer to a heated serving dish and keep warm. Strain the liquid into a small saucepan and reduce over a high heat until ⅓ remains. Remove from the heat and whisk in the remaining butter and when thick and foamy whisk in the lemon juice and pour over the mussels. Serve very hot with chunks of fresh crusty french bread. Serves 4.

Prawn-Filled Artichokes

6 large artichokes
water

The Dressing:

1½ cups mayonnaise
2 tablespoons white vinegar
½ tablespoon lemon juice
½ tablespoon anchovy sauce
1 small clove garlic, crushed
pinch of cayenne pepper
1 teaspoon chopped tarragon
2 tablespoons chopped parsley
3 tablespoons sherry

For Serving

500g (1lb) prawns shelled, chopped
¼ cup chopped shallots

Trim the artichokes so that they sit upright in a suitably sized saucepan. Cover with water and boil until tender. The artichokes are cooked when one of the leaves close to the top comes out easily when pulled with a pair of tongs. Remove from the heat and drain upside down until cooled.
Pull out the centre, leaving enough "wall" to support the shape of the artichoke. Make the dressing by combining all the ingredients together in a blender or food processor.
Pour over the combined prawns and shallots. Spoon into the artichokes and serve garnished with a sprig of herbs.
Serves 6.

Whole Stuffed Snapper

(Photograph this page)

The Stuffing:

1 tablespoon butter or margarine
1 onion, chopped
2 cups fresh breadcrumbs
grated rind and juice ½ lemon
1 tablespoon chopped parsley
½ cup chopped shallots

For Cooking:

4 x 500g (1lb) Schnapper
melted butter
lemon juice

Melt butter in a saucepan and sauté the onion until tender and stir into the combined remaining stuffing ingredients. Spoon into the cavity of the fish and secure the openings. Place in a shallow greased baking dish and pour over sufficient butter and lemon juice to coat the fish. Cover with foil and bake at 190°C (370°F) for 30-35 minutes or until cooked. Serve hot with the juices spooned over the fish.
Serves 4.

Savory Stuffed Trout

Fish prepared in this way are ideal cooked on the barbecue.

2 large trout

The Stuffing:

60g (2oz) fresh bread crumbed
¼ cup chopped onion
1 rasher bacon, chopped
grated rind ½ orange
¼ cup chopped fresh herbs
Seasoning to taste

Fill the cavity of the fish with the combined stuffing ingredients, secure opening and wrap each fish in a large square of buttered foil. Bake at 180°C (350°F) for approximately 20 minutes or until cooked. Serve garnished with slices of lemon and parsley.
Serves 2.

Prawn Cocktail

Any of the mayonnaise recipes from this section would make an ideal accompaniment to this recipe in particular the tomato mayonnaise from "Prawn Filled Tomatoes".

2 shallots, chopped
1kg (2lb) prawns, shelled
4 lettuce leaves, shredded
lemon wedges

Combine lettuce and shallots and divide between 6 cocktail dishes. Top with the prawns and serve garnished with lemon wedges.
Serves 6.

Photograph below:
Whole Stuffed Schnapper

Prawns in Fresh Tomato Sauce

This is delicious served as an entree.

30g (1oz) butter or margarine
1 onion, finely chopped
1 clove garlic, crushed
500g (1lb) ripe tomatoes, pureed
¼ teaspoon dried basil
½ cup dry white wine
1 tablespoon tomato paste
500g (1lb) prawns
1 tablespoon parsley, finely chopped
1 shallot, sliced
Seasoning to taste

Melt the butter in a frying pan, add the onions and garlic and sauté until onion is tender.
Add tomatoes, seasoning, basil, wine and tomato paste. Bring to the boil and simmer uncovered for 20 minutes until the sauce has reduced and thickened. Stir the prawns into the tomato sauce and simmer gently until heated through. Sprinkle with chopped parsley and shallot and serve with the hot fluffy rice.
Serves 4.

Prawn-Filled Tomatoes

Tomatoes filled with prawns can make an ideal main dish, or an accompaniment to salads.

6 tomatoes
½ cup chopped onion
2 teaspoons parsley
1 tablespoon tomato paste
chicken stock
1 cup mayonnaise
500g (1lb) king prawns, shelled, de-veined, chopped
¼ cup chopped celery
¼ cup chopped shallots

Cut a slice from the top of each tomato and scoop the pulp into a saucepan. Place tomatoes upside down on kitchen paper to drain and refrigerate. Make a tomato sauce by stirring the onion, parsley and tomato paste into the reserved pulp. Add sufficient stock to cover and boil rapidly until reduced and slightly thickened, strain into a bowl, cool and refrigerate. Stir sufficient tomato sauce into the mayonnaise to obtain a coating consistency. Toss the prawns, celery and shallots together into a bowl and spoon over the tomato mayonnaise, stir carefully to combine. Spoon into the tomato cases replacing lids and serve on a bed of watercress.
Serves 6.

Scallops, Broccoli with Garlic Sauce

3 tablespoons oil
1 onion, roughly chopped
2 cloves garlic, crushed
1 knob root ginger finely chopped
6 shallots, chopped
125g (4oz) mushrooms, sliced
250g (8oz) broccoli, into florets
230g (7oz) can* sliced bamboo shoots, drained
2 tablespoons soy sauce
1 teaspoon satay sauce
¾ cup beef stock
1 tablespoon cornflour
water to mix
500g (1lb) scallops

Heat oil in a frying pan, and sauté onions, garlic and ginger for approximately 2 minutes. Add the shallots, mushrooms, broccoli, bamboo shoots and cook a further 3 minutes then stir in the soy sauce, satay sauce and stock and allow to boil. Blend the cornflour with a little water, add to vegetables and stir until the sauce boils and thickens. Add scallops and simmer until just cooked.
Served with boiled rice.
Serves 4.
*Nearest equivalent can size.

Photograph above:
Work on oyster trays — Lake Wallis Victoria.

Photograph following pages 30/31.
Blessing of the Fleet — Fremantle, Western Australia

Trout Almondine

90g (3oz) butter
4 small trout
½ cup cream
2 tablespoons orange liqueur
2 tablespoons Cognac
½ cup almond flakes, toasted
Seasoning to taste.

Melt the butter in a frying pan and pan-fry the trout until cooked.
Warm the cream in a small saucepan but do not allow to boil. Stir in the liqueur, Cognac, and seasoning. Transfer trout to a serving platter. Pour over the sauce, garnish with almonds and serve.
Serves 4.

Oyster Volettes

An elegant passround to serve with drinks.

½ cup cream
¼ cup sour cream
1 small onion, finely chopped
¼ teaspoon salt
⅛ teaspoon cayenne pepper
24 frozen vol-au-vent cases, cooked
24 oysters
small jar black or red caviar

Combine the creams and whip until thick. Fold in the onion and seasonings. Spoon into cold pre-baked vol-au-vent cases and garnish with oysters and caviar.

Seafood Bowl

For individual serves, the pastry could be cut into 6 and used to line individual quiche tins.

8 shallots, chopped
1 clove garlic, crushed
30g (1oz) butter or margarine
375g (12oz) green prawns, shelled, de-veined
375g (12oz) scallops
¾ cup dry white wine
½ teaspoon salt
pinch cayenne pepper
2 tablespoons cornflour
½ cup cream
8 sheets frozen filo pastry, thawed
60g (2oz) butter or margarine, melted
½ cup grated Gruyere or Swiss cheese

Sauté the shallots and garlic in the butter. Add the prawns, scallops, wine and seasonings, bring to the boil and simmer uncovered for 1 minute. Gradually blend cornflour and cream to a smooth paste and stir into the prawns and scallops, bring to the boil and boil gently for 1 minute, stirring constantly. Brush each sheet of pastry with melted butter and layer. Line a lightly greased 18cm (7") x 20cm (8") quiche tin, folding the edges over or under to neaten. Spoon the prawn mixture into the pastry case and sprinkle with the cheese. Bake at 190°C (370°F) for 10 minutes or until cooked and brown.
Serves 6.

Photograph opposite page:
Shelling Scallops — Coles Bay, Tasmania

Coquilles St. Jacques

¾ cup white wine
4 shallots, finely chopped
500g (1lb) scallops
2 tablespoons butter
1 tablespoon flour
1 cup cream
½ cup grated Parmesan cheese
½ cup fresh breadcrumbs
2 tablespoons melted butter
Seasoning to taste.

Heat the wine, shallots and seasoning in a saucepan until boiling. Add the scallops, remove from the heat, cover and stand for 5 minutes. remove scallops with a slotted spoon and divide between 4 scallops shells. Continue to cook the wine mixture over a high heat until reduced to ¼ cup. Make a sauce in the usual way with the butter, flour and cream. Stir in the wine and pour over the scallops. Combine the Parmesan cheese with the breadcrumbs and melted butter and divide equally between the shells. Grill until lightly browned and serve at once.
Serves 4.

Redfish Fillets in Zucchini Cream

1½ teaspoons butter or margarine
500g (1lb) redfish fillets
½ cup sliced zucchini
⅓ cup buttermilk
1½ tablespoons sour cream
seasoning to taste
Melt the butter in a frying pan and gently fry the fish until lightly golden, approximately 4 minutes. Remove from the pan and keep warm. Saute the zucchini in the same pan until cooked but still crisp, then stir in the buttermilk, sour cream and seasoning.
To serve, pour the zucchini cream over the red fish fillets and serve on a bed of lightly steamed leeks and carrot straws.
Serves 4.

Photograph below:
Lifesavers in Surf Boat Race, Manly, New South Wales.

Trout with Almonds and Crabmeat Stuffing

(Photograph this page)

This fish is probably regarded as one of the greatest in the world, and with its delicate fine texture, and the combination of crabmeat, makes for a delicious meal.

6 trout
⅓ cup rice
30g (1oz) butter or margarine
4 shallots, chopped
90g (3oz) mushrooms, chopped
1 x 220g (7oz) can* crab, drained
1 teaspoon lemon juice
seasoning to taste
flour to coat
60g (2oz) almonds, browned in butter
*Nearest equivalent can size.

Wash and clean trout. Cook rice in pan of boiling salt water for 10 minutes or until tender, drain well. Melt the butter in a frying pan and sauté the shallots and mushrooms for 1 minute. Stir in the rice, crab, lemon juice and seasoning. Coat fish with flour and fill the cavity with the crabmeat stuffing. Secure opening to prevent filling from spilling out while frying. Panfry the trout until cooked and golden. Sprinkle with the almonds and serve.
Serves 6

Vegetables with Italian Mullet Filling

The Mullet Filling
400g mullet fillets, skinned, minced
1 onion finely chopped, sauteed
2 cloves garlic crushed, sauteed
¼ teaspoon dried thyme leaves
½ teaspoon dried basil leaves
2 tablespoons finely chopped parsley
1 tomato, skinned finely chopped
2 tablespoons tomato paste
10 black olives, seeded
seasoning to taste
choose either:-
2 eggplant
2 capsicums

Combine the ingredients for the filling in a bowl and mix well. Set aside whilst preparing your choice of vegetables.
Eggplant — cut eggplant in half lengthwise, remove flesh leaving a layer of 1cm (½") next to the skin. Finally chop the flesh and add to the mullet filling, mixing well. Pack the fish mixture back into each half.
Capsicum — cut capsicums in half lengthwise, removing seeds, par boil for approximately 5 minutes. Remove from the water and pack the fish mixture back into each half. Place each vegetable into a shallow ovenproof dish and bake at 180°C (350°F) for 20-25 minutes.

Lemon Whiting

Lemon poached whiting makes a delightful dish.

6 whole whiting
1 small onion, finely sliced
finely grated rind 1 lemon
¼ cup lemon juice
1¾ cups water
1 bayleaf
seasoning to taste

Cottage Cheese Accompaniment

1 tomato, sliced
1 lemon, sliced
1 x 200g (6-7oz) carton cottage cheese
finely grated rind 1 lemon
1 tablespoon lemon juice
salt, cayenne pepper, to taste
1 tablespoon chopped parsley

Arrange fish in the base of an electric frying pan with the remaining ingredients. Cover and simmer for 5 minutes or until the fish are just cooked. Using a slotted spoon, carefully remove fish onto a serving platter, and when cool, cover and refrigerate. Prepare the accompaniment by arranging the slices of tomato and lemon around the fish. Combine the remaining ingredients together and serve with the fish.

Deep-Fried Calamari

(Photograph this page)

This makes an excellent appetizer to serve with cocktails.

½ cup flour
½ cup self-raising flour
1 teaspoon salt
1 egg
½ cup water
1 tablespoon oil
1kg (2lb) squid
oil for frying
For serving tartare sauce,
lemon wedges

Make a batter by beating the flours and salt together in a bowl with the combined egg, water and oil. Prepare the squid by gently pulling the tentacles from the body. Rinse under running cold water until the ink is removed. Slide out the piece of cuttle which forms the backbone and peel the skin from the squid and cut the body into rings. Cut away and discard the hard sections from the tentacles. Cut tentacles and flat fins into strips. Dry thoroughly on kitchen paper. Heat the oil, dip the squid in the batter and deep-fry until golden brown. Drain and serve with tartare sauce and lemon wedges. Serves 4-6.

Mussels in Garlic Butter

(Photograph this page)

Mussels are always available in your local fish shop, here is something very quick and simple to do with them.

125g (4oz) butter or margarine, cubed
2 cloves garlic, crushed
¼ cup chopped parsley
2 dozen mussels, washed, beards removed
¼ cup chopped shallots
2 sprigs thyme
1 bay leaf
¼ teaspoon salt
1 cup dry white wine

Cream the butter with the garlic and parsley in a bowl, place the mussels in a saucepan with the remaining ingredients. Bring to the boil and simmer for 3 minutes or until the mussels open. Detach the lid from the base and place the mussels still sitting in the shell on a baking sheet. Dot generously with the garlic butter and grill until the butter has melted. Serves 2.

Seafood Vol-Au-Vent

1 packet frozen vol-au-vent cases
12 scallops
16 prawns, shelled, deveined
¼ cup water
28g (1oz) packet* white wine sauce mix
½ cup milk
1 tablespoon butter or margarine
1 jar oysters, well drained

*nearest equivalent packet size

Cook vol-au-vents as instructed on the packet and keep warm. Poach scallops and prawns in the water for 1 minute. Blend the sauce mix with the milk, add the seafood together with the butter, bring to the boil, reduce heat, simmer for 3 minutes, stirring constantly. Fold in the oysters, adjust seasoning if necessary and spoon into the vol-au-vent cases and serve garnished with a sprig of dill or fennel.
Serves 4.

Photograph below:
Calamari/Mussels in garlic butter

Flathead and Dill Butter in Filo Pastry

grated rind ½ lemon
6 sprigs dill
90g (3oz) butter, softened
12 sheets filo pastry
90g (3oz) butter, melted
6 large flathead fillets

Cream the lemon rind, dill and butter together. Brush 6 sheets of filo pastry with the melted butter and layer. Repeat with the remaining pastry. Spread ½ the lemon dill butter over each rectangle of pastry and divide each piece into 3 even strips lengthwise. Place a fillet of fish down the centre of each strip and fold into a neat parcel, sealing the edges. Place on a baking sheet, brush with melted butter and bake at 180°C (350°F) for 20-30 minutes, until cooked and golden.
Serves 6.

Crab au Gratin

(Photograph this page)

A special dish for entertaining when crabs are not too expensive.

4 small crabs
1 tablespoon chopped shallots
½ cup chopped mushrooms
1 tablespoon butter or margarine
2 tablespoons Cognac
Seasoning to taste.

Gratin Sauce:
2 tablespoons butter or margarine
2 tablespoons flour
1½ cups fish stock
½ cup cream
1 teaspoon French mustard
1 teaspoon cayenne pepper
½ cup grated cheese

Prepare crab meat in the usual way and set to one side, being careful to keep the shells intact. Sauté the shallots and mushrooms in the butter, season and pour over the warmed ignited Cognac. Remove from the heat. Make the sauce by melting the butter in a saucepan and stirring in the flour over a low heat for 1-2 minutes. Gradually add the fish stock and stir until the sauce thickens then stir in the cream, mustard and seasoning. Allow to simmer for 2-3 minutes then remove from heat and stir in the crab meat and mushrooms. Spoon the mixture into the crab shells, sprinkle with cheese and bake at 150°C (300°F) for 5 minutes.
Serves 4.

Citrus Microwave Fish

(Photograph page 36)
Fish just tastes so good cooked in the Microwave.
1.5kg (3oz) whole snapper
90g (3oz) butter or margarine
2 cloves garlic, crushed
freshly ground black pepper
pinch salt
250g (8oz) prawns, shelled, de-veined, chopped
125g (4oz) scallops
¼ cup chopped shallots
1 cup breadcrumbs
grated rind, lemon juice 1 orange

Place snapper in a shallow dish and dot with butter, cover with plastic wrap and Microwave on MEDIUM for 10 minutes and allow to stand. Melt the remaining butter on HIGH for approximately 1 minute, add garlic, black pepper and salt then stir in the prawns, scallops, shallots, breadcrumbs, orange rind and juice. Microwave on MEDIUM for 3 minutes, stirring once, and serve poured over the fish.
Serves 4.

Gemfish in Filo Pastry

2 tablespoons chopped dill
2 tablespoons chopped pine nuts
1 teaspoon grated lemon rind
½ teaspoon lemon pepper
90g (3oz) butter, melted
12 sheets filo pastry
6 gemfish fillets

Combine the dill, pine nuts, lemon rind, pepper and 2 tablespoons melted butter. Brush 6 sheets of filo pastry with the melted butter and layer. Repeat with remaining pastry and divide each piece into 3 even strips lengthwise.
Place a gemfish fillet on each strip of pastry and spread with some of the dill and nut butter. Fold each one into a neat parcel sealing the edges. Place on a baking sheet, brush with melted butter, bake at 180°C (350°F) for 20-30 minutes.
Serves 6.

Photograph opposite page:
Citrus Microwave Fish

Photograph below:
Crab Au Gratin

Fettucine, Smoked Trout and Maraschino

2 tablespoons garlic butter
410g (13oz) cooked fettucine
½ cup cream
2 smoked trout filleted, boned, flaked
¼ cup cherry liqueur
½ cup slivered almonds, toasted
Seasoning to taste.

Melt the butter in a frying pan and add the fettucine, cream, fish and liqueur. Stir all the ingredients together over a low heat until the sauce thickens, season and serve liberally sprinkled with the toasted almonds.
Serves 6.

Photograph following pages: 40/41
Surf Carnival — Sydney, New South Wales

Pages 42/43
Akuna Bay — Ku-ring-ai,
Sydney, New South Wales

Pages 44/45
Sydney from the air — New South Wales

Photograph opposite page:
Trawler at sea sorting prawns

Photograph below:
Mixed catch in Whisky Sauce

Chilli Prawns

Prawns are a favourite dish in Australia, and with the addition of fresh chilli to the recipe, it adds a delicious spicy flavour.

¼ cup tomato sauce
1 tablespoon sherry
1 tablespoon sugar
2 tablespoons oil
1 red chilli, seeded, finely chopped
2 cloves garlic, crushed
1 teaspoon finely chopped root ginger
6 shallots, chopped
750g (1½lb) green prawns, shelled, de-veined

Combine the tomato sauce with the sherry and sugar. Heat the oil in a wok over a medium heat, add the chilli, garlic and ginger. Stir in the shallots and tomato mixture. Simmer for 2-3 minutes, stirring occasionally. Add the prawns and simmer until just cooked. Serve on a bed of spaghetti, garnished with chopped parsley.
Serves 4.

Mixed Catch in Whisky Sauce

(Photograph this page)

Whisky particularly enhances seafood and adds a finishing touch to the sauce.

1 onion, roughly chopped
1 tablespoon butter or margarine
500g (1lb) large green prawns, shelled, de-veined
½ cup whisky
500g (1lb) white fish fillets
1-1½ cups dry white wine
1½-1¾ cups fish stock
2 tablespoons butter or margarine
2 tablespoons flour
¼-½ cup cream
salt and cayenne pepper to taste

Sauté the onion in the butter using a large frying pan with a lid. Add the prawns, warm the whisky, ignite and add to the pan. When the flames have subsided add the fish fillets and pour over the wine. Cover and simmer 3-5 minutes. Transfer the fish and prawns to a serving platter, cover and keep warm. Make the whisky sauce by adding the stock to the frying pan and whilst heating, cream the butter and flour together, gradually stir the creamed mixture into the stock and stir until smooth and slightly thickened. Add the cream and gently simmer for approximately 10 minutes. Season and pour over the fish just prior to serving.
Serves 4-6.

Baked Fish Tropical

A schnapper is an ideal fish used for this recipe and can also be cooked successfully in the Microwave.

2½kg (5lb) fish

The Stuffing:

1 cup cooked rice
1 tablespoon desiccated coconut
1 tablespoon chopped shallots
1 egg
1 teaspoon salt
1 teaspoon lemon pepper
2 tablespoons white wine

Fill the cavity of the fish with the combined stuffing ingredients. Secure opening and place the fish on a large piece of buttered foil. Wrap up into a secure parcel and bake at 180°C (350°F) for approximately 40-50 minutes or until cooked.

INSPIRED BY THE VINE

It is pleasing to see that not only cooks, but housewives too, have experienced the great advantages of using wine, not only in entertaining, but in cooking as well. There is no mystique about cooking with wine. In wine growing areas, wine is a natural local ingredient, which cooks through the ages have used to add an extra quality to their dishes. It rounds off the flavour of a dish, adding a richness and mellow quality.

Australia produces world class quality wines and our vineyards occupy 30 per cent of our total crop area. After World War II many thousands of migrants from Europe, influenced and encouraged production of dryer lighter wines, and now, 43 per cent of our grape crops are made into wines of all varieties.

One should ensure that there are good supplies of wine in the kitchen for cooking. Sherries, ports, marsalas and liqueurs as well as red and white wines, will enhance the flavour and tenderness of many recipes. Meat will become tender and succulent when marinated for a few hours in wine. Casseroles containing wine have their flavour enriched and strengthened by reheating. Seafood dishes, many sauces and desserts are also enhanced with the addition of wine or liqueurs.

Try these delicious recipes and see how easy it is to turn everyday dishes into an event with clever use of wine, nature's gift to man for more than 6,000 years.

Photograph opposite:
"Harvest Time."
Drayton's Vineyard.
Hunter Valley, New South Wales.

Fish Soup

1 onion, chopped
1 clove garlic, crushed
3 tablespoons oil
½ teaspoon thyme
½ teaspoon rosemary
500g (1lb) fish fillets, skinned, boned
seasoning to taste
2 tablespoons tomato paste
1 cup white wine
4 cups water
3 tablespoons brandy
1½ cups cream
3 tablespoons grated Parmesan cheese

Sauté the onion and garlic in the oil until tender. Add the herbs and chopped fish. Stir fry for 5 minutes. Season and stir in the tomato paste, white wine and water, simmer until the fish has cooked then stir in the brandy and cream; re-heat and serve with the Parmesan cheese.
Serves 8-10.

Coconut Scallops

A very simple way to serve scallops, but very delicious.

750g (1½lb) scallops
1 fresh coconut
1 tablespoon butter or margarine
3 tablespoons brandy
¾ cup cream
½ teaspoon salt

pinch cayenne pepper
4-6 cups cooked rice

Remove flesh from coconut and shred finely. Melt the butter in a frying pan, stir in the brandy and cream, increase the heat and add the coconut, salt and pepper; stir until the sauce has reduced and thickened, approximately 30 seconds - 1 minute. Stir in the scallops and when just cooked spoon onto hot saffron rice and serve.
Serves 6.

Fish Paté

500g (1lb) fish fillets, skinned, boned
1 shallot, chopped
grated rind ½ lemon
½ cup dry white wine
1 chicken stock cube
60g (2oz) butter or margarine
salt, cayenne pepper
⅓ cup cream
2 teaspoons lemon juice

Place fish, shallot, lemon rind, wine and stock cube into a pan. Simmer gently for 5 minutes or until fish is just tender. Puree the fish with the stock cube, butter, salt, cayenne pepper, cream and lemon juice until smooth and spoon into a serving bowl or 4 individual moulds. Refrigerate several hours. Serve with melba toast or savoury biscuits.
Serves 4.

Baked Mussels

(Photograph this page)
30 mussels
2 shallots, finely chopped
1 sprig thyme
2 sprigs parsley
1 bay leaf
½ teaspoon salt
½ cup white wine
125g (4oz) butter or margarine, softened
1 tablespoon parsley, chopped
2 cloves garlic, crushed
1 tablespoon chives

Scrape beard, scrub and wash mussels thoroughly and place in a large saucepan with the shallots, thyme, parsley and bayleaf. Sprinkle over salt and then add the wine. Steam for 5 minutes or until the shells have opened. Open mussels and discard lids. Divide mussels in remaining half shells into 4 ovenproof dishes. Make a herb butter by combining butter, parsley, garlic and chives and place a generous portion on each mussel. Bake at 190°C (370°F) for approximately 3 minutes or until butter has melted.
Serves 4.

Photograph below:
Baked Mussels

Rabbit Terrine

This would be wonderful packed in the picnic hamper, as it travels well.

500g (1lb) rabbit
250g (8oz) belly pork
1 onion
1 teaspoon chopped fresh thyme
1 tablespoon chopped parsley
1 clove garlic, crushed
seasoning to taste
¼ cup claret
¼ cup brandy
2 rashers bacon
1 bay leaf

Mince the rabbit with the pork and onion. Add herbs, garlic seasoning, wine and brandy and mix well. Press half the mixture into a greased terrine, cover with the bacon then top with remaining meat. Crumble the bay leaf over the top. Cover with foil and stand in a water bath, bake at 180°C (350°F) for 1½ hours. Cool, then refrigerate overnight.
Serves 6-8.

Aspic Garnish

(Photograph this page)
2 teaspoons gelatine
½ cup hot chicken stock
2 teaspoons lemon juice
1 tablespoon sherry
seasoning to taste

Dissolve the gelatine in the hot stock and stir in the remaining ingredients. Pour into the base of a wetted chilled mould and spoon in the paté of your choice. Refrigerate until set.

Pork Paté

(Photograph this page)

60g (2oz) butter or margarine
750g (1½lb) pork liver,
roughly chopped
3 rashers bacon, chopped
4 shallots, chopped
3 cloves garlic, crushed
350g (12oz) finely minced pork
seasoning to taste
pinch of each nutmeg, oregano
1 tablespoon brandy
1 cup hot beef stock
4 teaspoons gelatine

Melt the butter in a frying pan and sauté the liver with the bacon, shallots, garlic, pork and seasoning, for 15 minutes, stirring occasionally. Remove from the heat and stir in the brandy and ½ cup beef stock. Puree until smooth in a food processor. Dissolve the gelatine in the remaining stock and stir into the meat mixture. Pour into a chilled wetted mould and refrigerate until set. Serve with crackers and crusty Bread.

Sherry Paté

(Photograph this page)
125g (4oz) butter or margarine
1 small onion, finely chopped
500g (1lb) chicken livers
1½ cups chicken stock
¼ cup sherry
½ teaspoon paprika
¼ teaspoon allspice
¼ teaspoon salt
¼ teaspoon cayenne pepper
½ cup brandy
125g (4oz) cream cheese
5 teaspoons gelatine

Melt the butter in a frypan and sauté the onion and chicken livers for 15 minutes, stirring occasionally. Pour in ¾ of stock with the sherry, paprika, allspice, salt and cayenne pepper and simmer for a further 5 minutes. Remove from heat, add the brandy and cream cheese, puree the mixture in a food processor until smooth. Heat the remaining stock and use to disolve the gelatine. Add to the chicken liver mixture. Pour into a wetted mould and refrigerate until set. Turn out onto a serving platter and serve with fingers of hot buttered toast.
Serves 6-8.

Photograph opposite:
Coopering, Barossa Valley Vineyards, South Australia.

Photograph below: Paté and Aspic

Anchovy Dip

(Photograph this page)
This is a really delicious dip, don't be impatient reducing the cream, as the wait will be really worthwhile.

1½ cups cream
2 x 45g (2oz) cans* flat anchovies
3 cloves garlic, crushed
½ teaspoon ground black pepper
½ teaspoon chopped parsley

Pour the cream into a saucepan. Add the other ingredients and stir over a medium heat until the cream boils. Allow to reduce slightly. Cool and refrigerate. When the thickened dip has chilled completely, serve with crisp celery and water biscuits. Makes approximately 1½ cups.
*Nearest equivalent can size.

Chicken Liver and Hazelnut Paté

(Photograph this page)
60g (2oz) butter or margarine
½ onion
1 clove garlic, crushed
500g (1½lb) trimmed chicken livers
150ml (¼ pint) cream
3 tablespoons dry sherry
3 hard-boiled eggs, chopped
1 teaspoon oregano
½ teaspoon marjoram
½ cup chopped hazelnuts,
1 teaspoon chopped parsley
seasoning to taste

Melt the butter in a frying pan and sauté the onion until cooked. Add the garlic and the livers and cook until the livers are just pink in colour. Remove the pan from the heat and stir in all the ingredients with the exception of the nuts. Puree in a food processor. Stir in the nuts and transfer to a serving dish. Sprinkle with extra chopped hazelnuts and refrigerate until required.
Serves 6.

Stuffed Cucumbers

(Photograph this page)

2 cucumbers
250g (8oz) cream cheese, softened
¼ cup chopped pecans
dash of Tabasco sauce
¼ teaspoon salt

Skin the cucumbers, cut in half lengthwise; scoop out the seeds. Sprinkle with salt and leave to drain. Beat the cream cheese, pecans, Tabasco and salt together. Dry the cucumbers and spoon the cheese mixture into the centre of each half. Sprinkle with chopped parsley and refrigerate. When firm cut into slices to serve.
Serves approximately 12.

Smoked Turkey Terrine in Pastry

(Photograph this page)

A rather attractive way of using filo pastry with the combination of smoked turkey.

1kg (2lb) smoked turkey breast
4 shallots, chopped
3 tablespoons brandy
2 cups cream
2 eggs
1 teaspoon cayenne pepper
6 sheets filo pastry
60g (2oz) butter or margarine, melted

Combine the turkey, shallots, brandy, cream, eggs, and seasoning in a food processor. Brush each sheet of pastry with melted butter and use to line terrine. Spoon the turkey mixture into the terrine and cover with the overlapping pastry. Cut slits in the top to allow the steam to escape. Brush with a little beaten egg. Bake at 190°C (370°F) for approximately 40 minutes or until cooked. When cool, cut into slices and serve.
Serves 6-8.

Braised Stuffed Mushrooms

12 medium-sized mushrooms
500g (1lb) minced steak
seasoning to taste
4 shallots, chopped
1 teaspoon chopped basil
¼ teaspoon chopped sage
½ cup red wine
½ onion, finely chopped
2 sticks finely chopped celery
1 carrot, finely chopped
wheatgerm or flour for thickening
beef stock

Remove stalks from mushrooms and chop finely. Add to the steak with the seasoning, shallots, basil, sage and wine. Add sufficient thickening to make a firm mixture. With mushroom cap up, spoon in filling to form a dome shape. Scatter vegetables over the base of a casserole dish and place the mushrooms on top. Pour sufficient beef stock to half cover mushrooms, cover and bake at 180°C (350°F) for 20 minutes. Remove mushrooms and thicken the stock. Serve mushrooms with the sauce.
Serves 6.

Marinated Quail

This very small game bird, is usually very tender, and should therefore be cooked quickly as the flesh tends to be rather dry. Delightful served as an appetizer or main course.

2 cups chicken stock
1 cup dry white wine
2 whole cloves
1 small onion, chopped
1 bay leaf, crushed
½ teaspoon salt
½ teaspoon cayenne pepper
1 tablespoon olive oil
6 quail

Place all ingredients with the exception of quail into a saucepan and bring to the boil. Cut the birds in half and place in a large bowl and cover with the hot marinade. Cool and refrigerate overnight. Lift quail from the marinade and grill or barbecue basting constantly throughout the cooking time. Serve when cooked and the skin is deep brown and crisp, with a side salad.
Serves 6.

Photograph below: Steak with Capsicums.

Steak with Capsicums

(Photograph this page)
A favourite dish with everyone.

2 tablespoons oil
2 onions, chopped
2 green capsicums, sliced
2 red capsicums, sliced
1 tablespoon flour
1 tablespoon chopped parsley
1 x 425g (14oz) can* tomatoes
¼ cup riesling
1 teaspoon basil
seasoning to taste
4 x 500g (1lb) thinly cut steaks
½ cup grated Parmesan cheese

Heat oil and sauté the onion and capsicums until tender. Add flour, chopped parsley and tomatoes then stir in the wine, basil and seaoning. Simmer over a low heat while cooking the steaks. Serve the steaks with a little of the sauce poured over the top, sprinkled with Parmesan cheese.
Serves 4.
*Nearest equivalent can size.

Sherried Pork Chops with Pears

A delightful way of cooking pork chops. If fresh pears are not available, canned pears can be substitued and just added 10 minutes before completion of cooking to heat through.

6 pork chops
3 firm pears
4 tablespoons lemon juice
¼ cup firmly packed brown sugar
¼ teaspoon ground cinnamon
¼ cup dry sherry
2 tablespoons butter or margarine
1 teaspoon cornflour blended with 1 tablespoon water

Brown pork chops in a frying pan in their own fat. Transfer to a large baking dish. Cut each pear in half lengthwise, remove core and stem and arrange pears, cut side up, around the chops. Sprinkle meat and fruit with lemon juice. In a small bowl, combine the brown sugar and cinnamon. Sprinkle over the meat and fruit, together with the sherry. Place a small nob of butter on each pear and bake at 160°C (325°F) for 30-40 minutes. Pour pan juices into a small pan and thicken with the cornflour and serve with the chops and pears.
Serves 6.

*Photograph page 57:
Sealing Wine Cask, Pokolbin, New South Wales.*

Lamb Hot Pot

1kg (2lb) lean lamb, cubed
seasoned flour
3 tablespoons oil
4 small onions, sliced
1 clove garlic, crushed
1 x 440g (14oz) can* tomato soup
2 cups stock
2 tablespoons sherry
1 tablespoon brown sugar
1 tablespoon lemon juice
1 tablespoon Worcestershire sauce
1 teaspoon dry mustard
seasoning to taste
2 carrots, sliced
1 parsnip, sliced
4 sticks celery, sliced
1 red capsicum, sliced
1 green capsicum, sliced
2 tablespoons chopped parsley

Toss lamb in seasoned flour and brown in the oil with onion and garlic. Add remaining ingredients with the exception of the vegetables. Cover and simmer for 1 hour. Add vegetables, cover and simmer a further ½ hour, or until vegetables are tender. Serve with crusty bread and mashed potatoes.
Serves 4-5.
*Nearest equivalent can size.

Photograph below:
Bean Pot (Recipe page 61)

Rich Beef Casserole

This delicious rich beef casserole is enhanced with the addition of good red wine.

1kg (2lb) round or topside steak
2 tablespoons oil
30g (1oz) butter or margarine
3 rashes bacon, roughly chopped
2 oinions, roughly chopped
2 cloves garlic, crushed
4 tablespoons flour
1 cup beef stock
1½ cups red wine
1 bay leaf
½ teaspoon thyme
seasoning to taste
125g (4oz) mushrooms, sliced
¼ cup finely chopped parsley

Trim fat from meat and cut into cubes. Heat the butter in the oil and brown the meat. Remove meat from the pan and sautè the bacon, onion and garlic in the pan drippings. Stir in the flour and allow to brown. Remove from the heat, stir in stock, wine, bay leaf, thyme, seasoning. Return the meat to pan and simmer for approximately 1 hour or until meat is tender. Stir in the mushrooms; cook a further 15 minutes and serve sprinkled with parsley.
Serves 4-6.

Beef and Red Wine Pie

375g (12oz) packed puff pastry
1 tablespoon butter or margarine
500g (1lb) lean minced steak
2 medium onions, sliced
1 medium green capsicum, sliced
1 cup red wine
2 tablespoons tomato paste
pinch basil
pinch marjoram
seasoning to taste
2 tablespoons cornflour
2 tablespoons water
125g (4oz) Mozzarella cheese, grated
2 tomatoes, sliced
1 egg, lightly beaten

Use ⅔ of the pastry to line a 23cm (9″) greased pie plate. Melt butter in a saucepan, and brown the meat well. Add onions, capsicum, wine, tomato paste and seasonings. Simmer uncovered for 35 minutes or until most of the liquid has evaporated. Blend the cornflour with the water. Add to the meat and simmer for 2 minutes until thickened. Stir in half the cheese. Spoon meat into the pie plate and top with the tomato slices then sprinkle with remaining cheese. Brush edge of pastry with a little egg and cover pie with reserved pastry. Glaze and decorate with any left over pastry. Bake at 190°C (370°F) for 20-25 minutes or until cooked.
Serves 4-6

Savoury Apricots in Port

A tasty accompaniment to lamb, pork, veal or beef.

1 x 825g (24oz) can* apricot halves
¼ cup apricot juice
½ cup cider vinegar
½ teaspoon ground cloves
1 cinnamon stick
¾ cup port
1 tablespoon arrowroot

Drain apricot, reserving ¼ cup of juice and place in an ovenproof dish. Heat vinegar with cloves and cinnamon in a saucepan and remove from heat. Blend the arrowroot and apricot juice together and stir in the port. Gradually blend in the arrowroot mixture and return to the heat. Bring to the boil stirring constantly and allow to boil until mixture thickens. Pour over apricots and cook at 160°C (325°F) for 15-20 minutes. Serve with roast meats.
*Nearest equivalent can size.

Fillet of Beef Wellington

This is an elegant dish for a dinner party and quite easy to prepare.

1½kg (3lb) fillet of beef
seasoning to taste
60g (2oz) butter or margarine
¼ cup brandy
125g (4oz) peppered cream cheese
90g (3oz) liver paté
1 x 375g (12oz) packet frozen
puff pastry
1 egg lightly beaten

Rub fillet with seasoning and melt the butter in a large frying pan. Sear the beef over a high heat until brown on all sides. Warm brandy, ignite and pour over beef. Allow flames to subside, cool meat, then arrange the cheese over the top of the fillet. Combine the paté with the pan juices and spread over the top of the cheese. Roll out the pastry into a rectangle large enough to encase the beef and place the fillet down one side. Brush edges with the egg. Fold pastry over, sealing the edges forming a neat parcel. Slash the top of the pastry with a knife at intervals, glaze with remaining egg and bake at 220°C (440°F) for 15 minutes, then at 180°C (350°F) for 20-30 minutes. Serve cut into thick slices.
Serves 6.

Bean Pot

(Photograph page 60)
A quick and easy hearty starter.

1 tablespoon butter or margarine
125g (4oz) bacon pieces
2 large onions, chopped
1 clove garlic, crushed
1 x 140g (5oz) can* tomato paste
1¼ cups water
1 tablespoon vinegar
2 teaspoons brown sugar
2 teaspoons Worcestershire sauce
½ teaspoon dry mustard
2 x 440g (14oz) cans* three bean mix
1 tablespoon sherry

Melt butter in a saucepan and fry bacon, onions and garlic until tender. Add remaining ingredients, cover and simmer 20 minutes. Serve in deep soup bowls.
Serves 3-4.
*Nearest equivalent can size.

Photograph below:
Southern Vales Wine Co-op, Southern Vales, Victoria

Cheese Crusted Veal

1.5kg (3lb) piece veal
black pepper
1 onion, sliced
½ cup white wine
½ cup water
90g (3oz) tasty cheese grated
3 slices bread, crumbed
2 tablespoons finely chopped parsley

Place veal into a greased baking dish and sprinkle with black pepper; top with the onion and pour over the combined wine and water. Cover with foil and and bake at 180°C (350°F) for 2½ hours, basting occasionally. While meat is cooking prepare crusty topping. Combine the cheese with the breadcrumbs and parsley. Press into the meat and bake uncovered a further 30 minutes or until the meat is tender.
Serves 6-8.

Photograph pages 58/59:
Hazelmere Winery, Southern Vales, Victoria.

Photograph pages 62/63:
Collingrove Homestead, Barossa Valley, South Australia.

Photograph page 64:
St Hallett's Vineyard, McLaren Vale, South Australia.

Tagliatelle Italia

An excellent dish for a party.

The Sauce:

¼ cup olive oil
1 clove garlic, crushed
1 onion, chopped
500g (1lb) minced steak
1 tablespoon chopped parsley
1 teaspoon basil
½ teaspoon oregano
½ cup claret
1 cup water
1 x 250g (8oz) can* tomato paste
½ teaspoon salt
1 cup grated Parmesan cheese

For Cooking:

185g (6oz) green tagliatelle
185g (6oz) white tagliatelle

Heat oil and sauté the garlic and onion till tender. Add steak and sauté till browned. Add parsley, basil, oregano, claret, water, tomato paste and salt. Cover and simmer for 35 minutes. Boil tagliatelle noodles together in boiling water till firm but tender. Drain and serve with the sauce poured over, and top with the grated cheese.
Serves 4.
*Nearest equivalent can size.

Duckling in Lemon Sauce

The flavour of sherry and lemon juice cuts through the richness of the duck, making this an excellent dish for a dinner party.

1 duckling
seasoning to taste
⅔ cup sugar
2 tablespoons cornflour
½ cup water
1 cup lemon juice
¼ cup dry sherry

Wash and clean duckling under cold running water. Pat dry with paper towels and truss ready for roasting. Season. Place into a baking dish, cover with foil. Bake at 180°C (350°F) for 1½ hours, brushing occasionally with pan juices. Place the sugar and cornflour into a small saucepan and blend into a smooth paste with the water. Add lemon juice, sherry and seasoning, stir until sauce boils and thickens. Pour fat from baking dish and pour the sauce over the duck, continue cooking, uncovered, a further 30 minutes or until duck is tender, basting continually with the lemon sauce.
Serves 2-4.

Veal Rolls Provolone Cream Sauce

(Photograph this page)
6 thin fillets veal
4 tablespoons soft white breadcrumbs
2 tablespoons grated Parmesan cheese
60g (2oz) grated Provolone cheese
1 tablespoon chopped parsley
1 small clove garlic, crushed
1 egg, beaten
3 rashes bacon, halved
4 tablespoons olive oil
2 tablespoons flour
¼ cup sweet sherry
1 tablespoon tomato paste
1¼ cups water
½ teaspoon salt
½ teaspoon basil

Pound veal thinly. Combine breadcrumbs, cheeses, parsley, garlic and egg. Place a piece of bacon on veal fillets and spread with the cheese mixture, roll up and secure with toothpicks. Heat oil in a frying pan, add garlic and sauté meat until brown. Drain off all but 1 tablespoon oil. Stir in flour, sherry, tomato paste, water, basil and salt. Stir until boiling. Return meat to pan. Cover and simmer 20 minutes. Serve with vegetables of choice.
Serves 3-6.

Photograph opposite:
St. Hallett's Vineyard, McLaren Vale, South Australia

Veal and Mushrooms in Cream Sauce

The veal is greatly enhanced in flavour with this tasty mushroom wine sauce.

2 tablespoons oil
8 veal chops
60g (2oz) butter or margarine
8 shallots, chopped
185g (6oz) mushrooms, sliced
2 cloves garlic, crushed
3 tablespoons flour
1¼ cups chicken stock
1 cup white wine
½ cup cream
seasoning to taste
1 teaspoon fresh tarragon or
½ teaspoon dried tarragon

Heat oil in a frying pan and sauté the veal until browned. Transfer to an ovenproof dish. Add 30g (1oz) butter to the pan and sauté shallots mushrooms and garlic for approximately 1 minute, then spoon on top of the chops. Melt the remaining butter, add the flour and stir over the heat for a few minutes then add the stock and wine. Stir until boiling then reduce heat, *simmer 2 minutes. Add cream, seasoning and tarragon. Pour over chops, cover and bake at 180°C (350°F) for 40 minutes.*
Serves 4.

Photograph below:
Veal Rolls Provolone Cream Sauce.

Whole Sole with Mushroom and Wine Sauce

125g (4oz) button mushrooms
60g (2oz) butter or margarine
4 shallots, finely chopped
2 sticks of celery, finely chopped
4 whole sole or flounder
seasoning to taste
1 cup dry white wine
30g (1oz) butter or margarine
1 tablespoon flour
½ cup milk
¼ cup cream
2 teaspoons lemon juice

Remove stalks from mushrooms and finely chop. Melt butter in a frying pan, add mushroom caps and sauté 2-3 minutes then remove from the pan. Add vegetables and sauté 2 minutes. Place fish onto a buttered dish, large enough to hold the fish in a single layer. Season and spread with the mushroom mixture. Pour over the wine, cover with foil and bake 180°C (350°F), 15-20 minutes until fish is just firm to touch. Drain cooking liquid from pan and reserve, keep fish warm. Make a sauce in the usual way with the butter, flour and reserved cooking liquid. Stir in the milk and cream. Bring to the boil and stir until the sauce thickens. Season, add lemon juice and pour over fish. Serve topped with mushroom caps.
Serves 4.

Pork Fillet and Apricot Apple

An ideal recipe which can be prepared ahead of time and cooked just prior to serving.

6 pork fillets
1 cup chopped dried apricots
¼ cup chopped shallots
6 thin slices of ham
flour
60g (2oz) butter or margarine
2 tablespoons apricot brandy
2 tablespoons Cognac
3 tablespoons tomato puree
3 apples peeled, thickly sliced
1 cup chicken stock

Slice the fillet lengthwise and open out onto a board. Combine the apricots and shallots and spoon some onto each fillet. Top with a slice of ham, roll and secure with string. Toss in flour and sauté in the melted butter. Pour in the brandies, tomato puree. apples and stock. Simmer over a medium heat, stirring constantly to avoid the rolls catching on the base of the pan, and adjust seasonings. Remove string from pork rolls and serve with the sauce and vegetables of choice.
Serves 6.

Chicken and Cherries

The pale chicken, with the red cherries makes this an elegant combination when entertaining

6 large chicken fillets
flour
60g (2oz) butter or margarine
1 tablespoon oil
500g (1lb) white or red cherries
1 cup cream
½ cup white wine
seasoning to taste

Flatten the chicken fillets and dust in plain flour. Melt the butter and oil in a heavy-based frying pan lightly sauté the chicken fillets. Add the cherries, cream, wine and seasoning; allow to boil; reduce heat then simmer for 10 minutes. The sauce should be quite thick. Serve with the sauce spooned over the chicken with the cherries on top.
Serves 6.

Chicken with Caraway Seeds

12 chicken thighs
3 tablespoons caraway seeds
20g (7oz) butter or margarine melted
3 finely chopped shallots
½ cup white wine
seasoning to taste

Place thighs in a baking dish and brush with butter, sprinkle with caraway seeds and bake at 180°C (350°F) for approximately 50 minutes. Transfer to a serving dish and keep warm. Pour off excess fat, add shallots, wine; increase heat and boil for 3 minutes then add the remaining butter, stirring vigorously. Season and serve with the chicken.
Serves 6.

Photograph page 67:
Hahndorf Vineyards, McLaren Vale, South Australia.

Photograph page 71:
Chateau Tahbilk Cellars, Nagambie, Victoria

Photograph pages 72/73:
Mitchellton Winery, Nagambie, Victoria

Photograph pages 74/75:
Seppeltsfield Winery, Barossa Valley, South Australia

Photograph pages 76/77 (Recipes page 70)
Strawberry Cream Freeze, Chocolate Dipped Strawberries, Oranges and Meringue Topping, Poached Vermouth Pears, Pineapple Surprise.

Photograph below:
Wine tasting at "Montrose" near Mudgee, New South Wales

Veal Marengo

A very tasty and economical dish to make, it can be made ahead and reheated when required.

1½kg (3lb) stewing veal
3 tablespoons olive oil
1 onion, chopped
1 x 140g (5oz) can* tomato paste
1 tablespoon flour
1½ cups chicken stock
1 cup riesling
2 bay leaves
½ teaspoon thyme
½ teaspoon basil
12 small white onions
seasoning to taste
60g (2oz) butter or margarine
250g (8oz) mushrooms
4 tomatoes, skinned, halved

Cut veal into cubes and brown in the oil. Stir in onion and tomato paste and cook for 2 minutes then blend in the flour, chicken stock and wine. Add bay leaves, thyme, basil, seasoning. Cover and simmer 1 hour. Meanwhile sauté onions in butter till brown and tender, add mushrooms then stir into the veal. Stir in tomatoes and simmer a further 30 minutes. Serve with noodles tossed in butter and Parmesan cheese.
Serves 8.
*Nearest equivalent can size

Crunchy Chicken Bake

This is an economical tasty dish to serve at the weekend.

1 large, cooked chicken
30g (1oz) butter or margarine
2 tablespoons flour
1¾ cups milk
1 teaspoons French mustard
2 sticks celery, sliced
1 green capsicum, de-seeded, quartered
1 onion, quartered
3 tablespoons lemon juice
2 tablespoons dry sherry
6 slices stale bread, crumbed
2 tablespoons finely chopped parsley
90g (3oz) butter
¼ cup Parmesan cheese

Skin and bone chicken and chop flesh. Make a sauce in the usual way with the butter, flour and milk. Stir in the mustard, combine the chicken with the sauce, vegetables, lemon juice and seasoning and spoon into a greased ovenproof dish. Combine the breadcrumbs and parsley and sauté in the butter. Cool slightly then stir through the Parmesan cheese, sprinkle over the top of the casserole and bake bake at 180°C (350°F) for 30 minutes.
Serves 4-6.

Chicken and Plum Sauce

The tasty plum sauce adds a special flavour to this dish and very easy to prepare.

12 chicken thighs
1 cup water
1 cup white wine
1 bay leaf
500g (1lb) plums, seeds removed
¼ cup chopped onion
2 teaspoons chopped parsley
½ teaspoon garum marsala
2 teaspoons soy sauce
seasoning to taste
chilli sauce to taste

Place the chicken in a baking dish with the water, wine and bay leaf. Cover and cook at 180°C (350°F) for 40 minutes. Strain the liquid from the chicken into a large saucepan, add the plums, onion, parsley, garum marsala and soy sauce. Simmer until the plums are tender. Allow to cool, puree, return to saucepan and simmer until reduced and thickened. Season and stir in chilli sauce. Pour over the chicken and continue to cook at 180°C (350°F) until heated through. Serve with rice.
Serves 6.

Apricot Brandy Sponge Pudding

A steamed pudding is always a welcome winter dessert, serve with whipped cream.

125g (4oz) butter or margarine
½ cup caster sugar
2 eggs
1 cup self raising flour
pinch salt
⅓ cup milk
1 x 825g (24oz) can* apricot halves, drained
2 tablespoons brandy

Cream butter and sugar together until light and fluffy. Add the eggs one at a time beating well after each addition, then add flour and milk. Grease a 5 cup pudding basin and cover the base with approximately 8 apricot halves; spoon in the cake mixture, cover and steam for 1¼ hours or until cooked. Meanwhile puree the remaining apricots with the brandy and heat in a small saucepan and serve with the pudding.
Serves 6.
*Nearest equivalent can size.

Poached Vermouth Pears

(Photograph page 76)
6 large pears, peeled
grated rind 1 lemon
grated rind 1 orange
1 cup dry vermouth
1 cup caster sugar
¾ cup thickened cream, whipped

Place all the ingredients with the exception of cream into a saucepan. Add sufficient water to cover the pears, bring to the boil and simmer for 15 minutes. Remove from the heat, transfer to a bowl and refrigerate for at least 12 hours. Drain the pears and serve with the cream, decorate with some of the fruit left and and a sprig of mint.
Serves 6.

Pineapple Surprise

(Photograph page 76)

The pineapple can be marinated overnight and then drained thoroughly prior to serving through the cream. Keep the pineapple shells if wished and serve the mixture in the shells for an attractive dessert.

1 medium pineapple
1 packet marshmallows, chopped
1 teaspoon nutmeg
½ cup brandy
½ cup sugar
1¼ cups thickened cream, whipped

Cut the pineapple in half lengthwise and scoop out the pulp with a sharp knife removing the core; roughly chop into cubes reserving as much juice as possible. Transfer to a large bowl and stir in the marshmallows, nutmeg, brandy and sugar. Cover and refrigerate for at least 4 hours. Stir through the whipped cream and serve.
Serves 4-6.

Oranges and Meringue Topping

(Photograph page 77)

This sophisticated dessert is extremely easy to prepare and of course looks most impressive.

6 medium-large oranges
2 tablespoons raisins
3 tablespoons brandy
1 tablespoon sugar
3 egg whites
3 tablespoons caster sugar

Cut the top from each orange and scoop out the pulp using a sharp knife. Retain the shells and dice the fruit into a glass bowl. Add the sugar, raisins and brandy and leave to marinate for 6 hours. Make a stiff meringue the usual way with the egg whites and remaining sugar. Fill the shells with the fruit mixture and pipe some meringue on the top of each one. Bake at 230°C (475°F) for a few minutes until the meringue has browned.
Serve immediately.
Serves 6.

Photograph below:
Stanton and Killeen Wine Vats, Rutherglen, Victoria

LETS GO TROPICAL

Nothing quite stirs the imagination like visions of a tropical paradise — brilliant sunshine, gently swaying palms, blue tranquil seas, white sands and tropical fruit plantations. There are delightful holiday islands dotted along the coastline, along with the Great Barrier Reef, that spectacular eighth wonder of the world which encloses 8,000 square miles of sea. Imagine this idyllic setting and you have the lucky country — Australia — of which 45% lies in the tropics.

Australians naturally love cool foods when temperatures are hot and there is a host of delicious, cool ingredients available for mouth watering recipes. Tropical waters abound with exotic fish and crustaceans which naturally lend themselves to tasty dishes. Our tropical fruit is luscious — avocados, mangoes, paw paws, sugar bananas, rock-melons, pineapples and passionfruit may be used in an endless variety of recipes.

Tropical food is not only confined to Northern Australia, so whether you live in Rockhampton or Rottnest, Darwin or Dimboola you can enjoy the lush fruits and cool enticing dishes of the tropics. This chapter is devoted to mouth watering recipes such as Piquant Lemon Whiting, Prawns in Coconut Sauce, Chilled Paw Paw Souffle, Island Pineapple Rum and many more to be enjoyed in this wonderful tropical Australia.

Photograph opposite:
Tourists inspecting coral, Great Barrier Reef,
Queensland

Iced Cucumber Soup

1 large onion, sliced
sprig mint
1 teaspoon dill
seasoning to taste
5 cups chicken stock
2 large cucumbers, peeled, seeded, chopped
2 tablespoons cornflour
1 tablespoon water
1/3 cup sour cream
green food colouring — optional
extra cucumber slices and mint for garnish

Simmer onion with the mint, dill, seasoning and stock until tender. Add cucumbers and cook for a further 10 minutes. Puree mixture until smooth in a blender. Return to saucepan. Add cornflour blended with water and bring to boil and simmer, 2-3 minutes. Remove from heat and allow to cool.
Add sour cream and mint with green colouring if desired. Pour into a large serving bowl, cover and chill. Serve garnished with cucumber slices and mint.
Serves 10.

Cherry Soup

A rather nice chilled fruit soup, making excellent use of fresh cherries.

500g (1lb) fresh cherries with their stalks
3 cups white wine
grated rind 1 lemon
juice 1 lemon
1 cinnamon stick
1/3 cup sour cream
3/4 cup cream
1/3 cup Cherry Advokat liqueur

Stone the cherries and leave to one side. Crack the stones and put them into a saucepan together with the stalks, wine, rind, juice and cinnamon. Bring to the boil and cook for 5 minutes; remove from the heat and allow to stand for 20 minutes. Strain and pour the juices into a saucepan; bring to the boil and add the cherries. Cook for 1 minute then remove from the heat. Pour in the creams and the liqueur. Stir well, cool and refrigerate. Serve well chilled.
Serves 6-8.

Photograph this page:
Beetroot with Sour Cream and Chives

Photograph opposite:
Chilled Fruit Soup (Recipe this page)

Chilled Fruit Soup

(Photograph page 80)
A refreshing cold summer soup.

1 large rockmelon
2 teaspoons lemon juice
1/2 cup cold water
1 chicken stock cube, crumbed
1 tablespoon orange liqueur
freshly ground pepper
6 chives, chopped

Peel, seed and cube rockmelon. Place half the rockmelon into a food processor and puree. Repeat with remaining rockmelon and pour into a bowl. Combine rockmelon puree, lemon juice, cold water, crumbled stock cube, liqueur, pepper and nutmeg. Stir thoroughly. Place in the refrigerator and chill for several hours before serving. Sprinkle with finely chopped chives and serve.
Serves 6.

Beetroot with Sour Cream and Chives

(Photograph this page)
This dish may be served hot as a vegetable or cold as a salad.

4 beetroot
1/2 cup sour cream
2 teaspoons lemon juice
1 teaspoon sugar
seasoning to taste
8 chives, chopped

Cook whole beetroot in boiling salted water until tender, approximately 1 hour. Drain, cool and skin. Slice the beetroot into thin strips, place into a bowl and chill. Combine the sour cream, lemon juice, sugar and seasoning in a bowl. To serve, spoon sour cream mixture over beetroot and sprinkle with chives.
Serves 6.

Avocado and Smoked Turkey Breast Salad

(Photograph this page)

A lovely mayonnaise to accompany turkey and avocado salad.

1 kiwi fruit, pureed
1 teaspoon curry powder
1 teaspoon mayonnaise
500g (1lb) smoked turkey breast, sliced
2-3 medium ripe avocados, peeled, sliced
6 sprigs of dill
kiwi fruit slices for garnish

Stir the kiwi fruit puree, and curry powder into the mayonnaise, mix well and refrigerate. Arrange the turkey breast and avocado slices alternately on a serving plate. Serve with the kiwi fruit mayonnaise and garnish with sprigs of dill and slices of kiwi fruit.
Serves 6.

Savoury Rice Mould

¼ cup raisins, chopped
1 green capsicum, de-seeded, roughly chopped
¼ cup parsley, chopped
¼ cup walnuts, roughly chopped
¾ cup canned pineapple pieces, drained, chopped
1 red apple, cored, chopped
1¼ cups long grain rice, cooked
½ cup oil
½ cup vinegar
2 teaspoons curry powder

Combine raisins, capsicum, parsley, walnuts, fruit and rice. Stir in the combined oil, vinegar and curry powder. Press mixture into a 20cm (8") ring mould and refrigerate for several hours. Serve unmoulded on to a plate, cut into wedges.
Serves 6-8.

Minted Orange Salad

A tangy mint dressing to accompany chilled fresh fruit.

6 oranges, peeled, halved, seeds removed
½ pineapple, peeled, cored, quartered
¼ cup mint leaves, chopped
2 teaspoons sugar
⅓ cup malt vinegar
2 tablespoons water

Slice the oranges and the pineapple into a serving bowl, and chill. Combine the mint, sugar, vinegar and water together in a blender until smooth. Pour dressing over oranges, toss and serve.
Serves 8-10.

Photograph opposite:
Pork and Melon Salad (Recipe page 86)

Photograph below:
Avocado and Smoked Turkey Breast Salad

French Dressing

(photograph page 96)
3 tablespoons white vinegar
2 tablespoons oil
¼ teaspoon powdered mustard
¼ teaspoon sugar
1 tablespoon chopped parsley
½ clove garlic
seasoning to taste

Blend all the ingredients together in a food processor and use as desired.

Creamy Blue Cheese Dressing

This tangy dressing is delicious served with a crisp green salad.

6 chives
¼ cup sour cream
125g (4oz) blue vein cheese
2 tablespoons mayonnaise
3 tablespoons milk
½ teaspoon prepared English mustard
1 teaspoon lemon juice
seasoning to taste

Combine all the ingredients in a food processor until smooth and creamy. Serve chilled.

Lychee Noodle Chicken

30g (1oz) butter or margarine
1kg (2lb) chicken portions
1 packet chicken noodle soup
1 x 425g (10oz) can* lychees, undrained
1 x 425g (10oz) can* crushed pineapple, undrained
1 tablespoon soy sauce
1 tablespoon cornflour
½ cup water
*Nearest equivalent can size.

Melt the butter in a frying pan and sauté the chicken pieces until brown; transfer to a casserole dish. Combine the soup mix, lychees, pineapple and soy sauce and pour over the chicken. Bake at 180°C (350°F) for approximately 20 minutes or until chicken is cooked. Combine the cornflour with the water, stir into the casserole and cook a further 15-20 minutes.
Serves 4.

Tropical Kebabs

Sauce:

3 tablespoons tomato sauce
1 tablespoon Worcestershire sauce
3 tablespoons Hoi Sin sauce
1 tablespoon lemon juice
2 tablespoons pineapple juice

1 onion, quartered
1 x 450g (16oz) can* ham, cubed
1 medium pineapple, cubed
250g (8oz) button mushrooms
1 green capsicum, de-seeded, quartered
1 red capsicum, de-seeded, quartered
*Nearest equivalent can size.

Combine all the sauce ingredients together in a jug. Alternate onion, ham, pineapple, mushrooms and capsicums onto presoaked skewers, allowing approximately 2 skewers per person. Baste the kebabs with the sauce and barbeque; continue basting during cooking. Serve on a bed of rice, garnished with parsley.
Serves 6.

Smoked Turkey and Honeydew Melon

Pernod Dressing:

3 egg yolks
½ teaspoon salt
¼ teaspoon cayenne pepper
1½ cups oil
½ mango, peeled, sliced
2 tablespoons Pernod

For Serving:

watercress
24 thin slices honeydew melon
24 slices smoked turkey breast

Make the Pernod Dressing by dropping the egg yolks into a food processor or blender with the salt and pepper. Process for 30 seconds and then add the oil in a continuous stream until a smooth consistency is obtained. Add the mango and Pernod and when smooth pour into a bowl and refrigerate. Alternate slices of melon and turkey on a serving platter and serve with the dressing.
Serves 6-8.

Ginger Chicken and Pineapple Salad

(photograph page 94/95)
Chicken and fruit make an excellent combination for a summer salad.

1 pineapple
1 large cooked chicken
small nob root ginger, grated
1 small onion, sliced
1 red capsicum, sliced
¼ cup grapes
¼ cup chopped parsley
herbed French dressing

Slice pineapple in half lengthwise and carefully remove flesh cutting into large cubes. Bone chicken and cut flesh into bite-size pieces. Combine the ginger with the onion, capsicum, grapes and parsley and finely stir in the chicken. Spoon back into the pineapple shells, sprinkle with dressing and serve well chilled.
Serves 6.

Sunshine Salad

(Photograph this page)
A refreshing colourful summer salad, which takes only minutes to prepare.

1½ cups cooked macaroni
1 cup sliced green beans
½ red capsicum, finely sliced
½ cup celery, finely sliced
¼ cup chopped shallots
2 tablespoons mayonnaise
shredded lettuce for serving

Combine all the ingredients in a large salad bowl and toss thoroughly. Chill until required. Serve on a bed of shredded lettuce.
Serves 2.

Photograph page 86:
Marinated Fruits (Recipe page 101)

Photograph page 87:
Start of the Sydney to Hobart Yacht Race, Sydney Harbour.

Photograph opposite:
North Queensland, Fishing Village

Photograph below:
Sunshine Salad.

Tropical Vegetable Pie

90g (3oz) butter, melted
1½ cups cracker biscuit crumbs
2 eggs, lightly beaten
⅓ cup milk
seasoning to taste
½ teaspoon ground thyme
1 cup grated Edam cheese
2 small zucchini, finely chopped
1 tablespoon parsley, chopped
1 tablespoon Parmesan cheese

Combine the melted butter and biscuit crumbs; press onto the base and sides of a 23cm (9") pie dish, chill until firm. Combine the eggs, milk, seasoning and thyme. Alternate layers of Edam cheese, zucchini in the pie shell, sprinkle with parsley and pour over the liquid. Top with Parmesan cheese and bake at 180°C (350°F) oven for 20-25 minutes. Serves 4-6.

Photograph below:
Crab Fisherman, Townsville, Queensland

Pork 'N' Orange Sauté

2 tablespoons butter or margarine
500g (1lb) pork fillet, cut into strips
1 cup chopped shallots
1 cup strained fresh orange juice
½ cup green ginger wine
1 tablespoon cornflour
1 cup thinly sliced celery
¼ cup almond halves

Melt the butter in a heavy based frying pan. Sauté pork and shallots for 5 minutes. Stir in orange juice. Cover and simmer for a further 5 minutes then blend in the ginger wine and cornflour. Stir until boiling then add celery and almonds and cook for 2-3 minutes. Spoon into serving dish and serve garnished with a few strips of orange rind. Serves 4.

Photograph opposite:
Yachting Brisbane River, Queensland

Photograph pages 90/91:
Sunset, Cairns, North Queensland

Mixed Tossed Salad

1 lettuce
3 tomatoes
½ cucumber
1 onion, sliced
8 radishes, sliced
125g (4oz) mushrooms
1 capsicum, sliced
3 sticks celery, sliced
French dressing

Wash and dry lettuce leaves and tear into bite-size pieces. Place into a large salad bowl with tomatoes cut into wedges. Score unpeeled cucumber with a fork and slice. Combine cucumber, onion, radishes, mushrooms, capsicum and celery in the bowl. Toss in French dressing and serve. Serves 6-8.

Salad of Two Pears

The delicate flavour of pears and avocados combine beautifully together.

⅓ cup oil
⅔ cup lemon juice
seasoning to taste
1 clove garlic, crushed
3 pears peeled, diced
3 avocados, peeled, diced

Make the dressing by combining the oil, lemon juice, seasoning and garlic. Carefully toss the pears and avocados in the dressing and spoon into lettuce cups to serve. Serves 6.

Avocado Green and Gold

A very colourful and refreshing salad.

2 avocados
2 teaspoons lemon juice
2 oranges
2 grapefruit
2 tablespoons oil
1 tablespoon vinegar
seasoning to taste
lettuce leaves, for serving

Cut avocados in half and carefully remove the seed. Sprinkle the cut surface with lemon juice to avoid discolouration. Remove skin and pith from the oranges and grapefruit and carefully segment. Mix the two fruits together with oil, vinegar and seasoning. Pile into avocados and chill for 1 hour. Serve on a bed of lettuce. Serves 2.

Avocado Crab Supreme

A sumptuous luncheon dish to impress your friends.

1 egg yolk
½ teaspoon salt
pinch cayenne pepper
1 tablespoon tarragon vinegar
⅓ cup oil
¼ teaspoon Tabasco sauce
1 teaspoon Worcestershire sauce
½ teaspoon lemon juice
½ cup cream, whipped
½ cup finely chopped capsicum
½ cup finely chopped shallots
1 x 170g (5oz) can* crabmeat, drained
1 avocado, peeled, sliced
¼ cup finely chopped ham
1 clove garlic, crushed
¼ cup chopped parsley
*Nearest equivalent can size.

Combine egg yolk, salt, cayenne pepper and vinegar in a blender. Whisk together oil, Tabasco sauce and Worcestershire sauce and gradually add to egg mixture. Blend until thickened. Fold in lemon juice, cream, capsicum, shallots and crabmeat. Spoon mixture into four ramekins and arrange avocado on top. Combine ham, garlic and parsley, sprinkle over ramekins, serve garnished with twists of lemon.
Serves 4.

Prawn Tropical

1 tablespoon finely chopped green capsicum
1 tablespoon finely chopped red capsicum
seasoning to taste
dash Tabasco sauce
1 quantity seafood sauce — (see recipe below)
2 avocados
juice ½ lemon
125g (4oz) prawns, shelled, deveined
lemon slices
parsley

Stir capsicum, seasoning and Tabasco into seafood sauce. Halve and stone avocados and brush with lemon juice. Arrange prawns in the centre of each avocado, spooning some of the seafood sauce over the top. Serve garnished with lemon and parsley.

Seafood Sauce:

¼ cup mayonnaise
2 teaspoons tomato sauce
¼ cup cream
seasoning to taste
1 teaspoon Worcestershire sauce

Blend all ingredients together to make a smooth sauce.
Serves 2.

Sesame Seafood Morsels

500g (1lb) fish fillets, skinned
2 tablespoons sesame seeds, toasted
1½ cups breadcrumbs
seasoned flour
2 eggs, beaten
125g (4oz) butter or margarine
4 cloves garlic, crushed
1 bay leaf, crumbled

Cut fish into bite-size pieces. Combine sesame seeds with breadcrumbs. Crumb fish pieces by tossing lightly in flour, dipping in egg, then finally tossing in sesame crumbs. Melt butter in a frying pan with garlic and bay leaf. Add fish and cook until crisp and golden. Drain and serve piled into a napkin lined basket.
Serves 4.

Prawn Parcels

Delicious served as an entree or with cool summer drinks

2 sheets frozen ready rolled puff pastry, thawed
8 large green prawns, deveined, butterflied
¾ cup dessicated coconut
¾ cup breadcrumbs
¼ cup chopped chives
lemon juice to moisten
seasoning to taste

Divide each sheet of pastry into 4 squares, placing a prawn in the centre of each one. Combine the coconut, breadcrumbs, chives, lemon juice and seasoning and spread some of this mixture over each prawn. Fold prawn over to re-shape, moisten the edges of the pastry and fold to completely encase the prawn. Make an X on the top of each pastry parcel. Place on a baking sheet and bake at 180°C (350°F) for approximately 10 minutes or until cooked and golden.
Serves 6.

Prawns in Curried Coconut Sauce

¼ cup dessicated coconut
¾ cup milk
1 onion
1 clove garlic, crushed
1 teaspoon finely chopped root ginger
1 tablespoon curry powder
1 tablespoon butter or margarine
1 tomato, peeled, chopped
1 teaspoon salt
500g (1lb) cooked prawns, shelled
1 tablespoon chopped fresh mint

Simmer coconut in milk, blend and strain, reserving liquid and a ¼ cup coconut. Combine onion, garlic, ginger, curry powder and butter in a saucepan and cook 2 minutes over a low heat. Add tomato, salt, reserved coconut and liquid, prawns and mint and heat through. Serve with rice.
Serves 4.

Fish Kebabs Indienne

8 fish fillets
4 firm bananas
1-2 teaspoons curry powder
¼ teaspoon nutmeg
1 x 170g (5oz) can* evaporated milk
2 tablespoons lemon juice
seasoning to taste
*Nearest equivalent can size.

Trim fillets, peel the bananas and cut each into four. Thread two fish fillets and 4 pieces of banana onto skewers and place in a shallow dish. Combine the remaining ingredients and pour over the kebabs. Refrigerate for 1 hour. Grill kebabs, basting them with the marinade during cooking and serve with boiled rice and tossed green salad.
Serves 4.

Flambé Fruits

60g (2oz) butter
½ cup caster sugar
1 x 425g (13oz) can* peach halves,
drained, syrup reserved
3 medium pears, peeled, thickly sliced
1 punnet strawberries, hulled
¼ cup Cognac
*Nearest equivalent can size.

Melt butter in large frying pan. Stir in sugar, allow to dissolve then add ½ cup reserved peach syrup. Stir until boiling, then add pears, peaches and strawberries; allow to heat through. Heat the Cognac in a small pan or ladle, ignite and pour over the fruits. Serve immediately with scoops of ice cream or whipped cream.
Serves 6.

Variations:

Cherries . . . Use 2 x 425g (13oz) cans* pitted cherries. Add the syrup, substitute Maraschino liqueur instead of Cognac.
Pineapple and Orange . . . Use 3 medium, peeled, sliced oranges and 1 x 425g (13oz) can* pineapple rings. Add the syrup, substitute Kirsch liqueur instead of the Cognac.

Pineapple & Creme De Menthe Sorbet

(Photograph page 101)
A brandy snap or sweet biscuit can be served with this dessert.

470g (15oz) can* pineapple, drained
1 tablespoon Creme de Menthe
1 tablespoon caster sugar
8 ice cubes
*Nearest equivalent can size.

Place all ingredients with the exception of the ice cubes into a blender and blend until smooth. With motor running, remove cover insert and add ice cubes, one at a time and continue blending until the mixture is smooth. Pour into an ice-cream tray and freeze. Allow to soften slightly and serve in parfait glasses decorated with a mint leaf.

Photograph pages 94/95:
Ginger, Chicken and Pineapple Salad (Recipe page 85)

Rockmelon Mousse

This looks very attractive decorated with whipped cream and extra rockmelon balls.

1 medium rockmelon, cubed
3 teaspoons gelatine
2 tablespoons boiling water
2 tablespoons orange juice
½ cup whipped cream
2 passionfruit

Puree the rockmelon in a food processor. Transfer to a bowl. Dissolve gelatine in boiling water, cool and add to rockmelon together with orange juice and then fold in the cream and passionfruit. Pour into one large serving dish or individual glasses. Refrigerate until set.
Serves 4-6.

Photograph below:
Flambé Fruits (Recipe this page)

Fruit Salad Ice Cream

½ small pineapple, finely chopped
2 bananas, mashed
6-8 cherries, pitted, chopped
¾ cup orange juice
2 tablespoons lemon juice
¾ cup sugar
2 teaspoons gelatine
¼ cup water
2 cups cream, whipped
½ cup evaporated milk, chilled
overnight, whipped
1 teaspoon vanilla essence
4 passionfruit

Combine the fruits in a large bowl and stir in the fruit juices. Dissolve the sugar and gelatine in the water, in a saucepan over a low heat, allow to cool, then stir into the fruit. Combine the cream, evaporated milk, vanilla and passionfruit pulp, stir through the fruit and transfer to a 2 litre (½gal) ice cream container and freeze. When semi-frozen, stir with a fork and re-freeze.

Strawberry Cream Freeze

(Photograph page 100)
2 eggs, separated
¼ cup caster sugar
3 teaspoons gelatine
¼ cup hot water
2 tablespoons strawberry jam
1 cup, lightly whipped, cream
250g (8oz) strawberries, hulled

Combine egg yolks and sugar and beat until thick and creamy. Dissolve the gelatine in hot water and while still hot add to the egg and sugar mixture, beating until well combined. Stir the gelatine mixture and the strawberry jam into the cream. Whip the egg whites stiffly, fold into the mixture and spoon into a dish, ready for freezing. Roughly chop the strawberries and swirl into the mixture. Freeze overnight and serve sliced, with wafers.
Serves 6-8.

Vanilla Ice Cream

1 x 400g (13oz) can* condensed milk
1 cup water
2 teaspoons vanilla essence
pinch salt
1 cup whipped cream
*Nearest equivalent can size.

Combine the condensed milk, water, vanilla and salt in a food processor; fold in the cream and transfer to a 1 litre (¼gal) ice cream container; freeze until almost set. Return mixture to food processor to break down any ice which may have formed in the mixture. Re-freeze until required.

Photograph above:
"Fisheye" view, Great Barrier Reef, Queensland

Cointreau Ice Cream

3 eggs separated
½ cup caster sugar
2 tablespoons Cointreau
2 tablespoons water
1⅓ cups cream, whipped

Beat the egg yolks, with the sugar, Cointreau and water in a double saucepan until light and fluffy. Cool. Beat the egg whites until stiff, fold into the Cointreau mixture with the cream and pour into a 20cm (8") square cake tin. Place in the freezer and freeze until partially set, then break up the mixture gently with a fork. Re-freeze in the tin until set.

Apricot Brandy Nectarines

A rich delicious dessert.

12 medium nectarines
½ cup sugar
3 egg yolks
1 tablespoon caster sugar
1 tablespoon wine
2 tablespoons Apricot Brandy

Poach the nectarines with ¼ cup sugar and sufficent water to cover. Make the sauce by combining the egg yolks, remaining sugar, wine and Apricot Brandy in the top of a double saucepan. Whisk over a medium heat until thick and frothy. Spoon over the nectarines and serve.
Serves 6.

Splendid Glazed Oranges

A splendid dessert for a hot summers day.

6 large oranges
3 tablespoons mandarin or orange liqueur
1½ cups sugar
½ cup water

Peel the oranges and cut the skin into julienne strips. Simmer in water for 10 minutes or until tender. Drain, and dry on absorbent paper. Transfer to a small bowl and marinate in the liqueur. Remove pith from the oranges, cut a slice from one end so they will stand and arrange in a serving dish. Boil the sugar and water in a saucepan until a firm ball stage is reached. (120°C (250°F) is using a jam thermometer). Add 3 tablespoons of the syrup to the orange peel and slowly glaze the oranges with the remaining syrup using a tablespoon at a time. Chill for several hours. Spoon the orange peel and marinade over the oranges and serve with whipped cream.
Serves 6.

Coffee Brazil Souffles

A rich, mouth-watering dessert.

60g (2oz) cooking chocolate, grated
1 tablespoon water
3 tablespoons Tia Maria
4 eggs, separated
2 tablespoons instant coffee
½ cup caster sugar
1¼ cups cream, whipped
1 teaspoon cocoa
1 tablespoon icing sugar

Melt the chocolate in the water with Tia Maria and allow to cool. Stiffly beat the egg whites, then beat the egg yolks, coffee and sugar together until well combined. Stir in the chocolate and fold in the egg whites and the cream. Spoon into individual serving dishes and refrigerate for at least 4 hours. Mix cocoa and icing sugar together. Sprinkle over each souffle before serving.
Serves 6.

Lime Daiquiri

(Photograph this page)

Daiquiris of all flavours can be made using the fruits of summer.

8 ice cubes
1 tablespoon rum
¼ cup lime juice
a little sugar, if required

Place all the ingredients into a blender and process until thick and frothy. Pour into a goblet and serve. Serves 1.

Island Pineapple Rum

1½ tablespoons white rum
1½ tablespoons Advokat
½ cup unsweetened pineapple juice
1 cup crushed ice

Shake all the ingredients together and strain into a chilled wine goblet. Garnish with spear of pineapple. Serves 1.

Tropical Tea

A refreshing drink for the tropics.

4 cups orange juice
4 tea bags
¼ cup lemon juice
3 pieces cinnamon stick
8 whole cloves
dash ground nutmeg
4 lemon slices for garnish

Bring orange juice to the boil in a saucepan. Remove from heat and add all other ingredients with the exception of the lemon slices. Cover and let steep 5 minutes or until desired strength. Remove tea bags. Allow to cool then chill. Strain and serve in small goblets garnished with lemon.
Serves 6-8.

Photograph opposite:
Tropical Orange Freeze (Recipe page 101)

Photograph below:
Lime Daiquiri (Recipe this page)
Orange Cocktail (Recipe page 101)

Banana Smoothie

1 banana
½ cup buttermilk or yoghurt
½ cup orange juice
1 tablespoon honey
1 tablespoon Ameretto
⅔ cup finely crushed ice

Blend all ingredients together in a food processor and pour into a tall milk shake glass. Serve with straws. Serves 1.

Photograph pages 104/105:
Rent-a-Yacht, Whitsunday Passage, Queensland.

Photograph pages 106/107:
Gove Peninsula, Northern Australia.

Photograph pages 108/109:
Clockwise: Spiced Pears (Recipe page 100), Kirsch Pineapple (Recipe page 101), Chocolate Cheese Cake (Recipe page 261), Jamaican Bananas (Recipe page 100).

FROM THE PLAINS PADDOCKS AND PASTURES

Since the pioneering days, meat has been an important part of the Australian diet. The most popular being grills, barbeques, casseroles and the traditional roast. With the abundance of great tasting beef, veal, lamb and pork, there are unlimited tasty dishes to be made. As meat becomes more expensive, the average Australian has to make a careful choice when purchasing meat, to gain the very best value from it. Our European migrants have shown us how to use aromatic herbs or creamy sauces to get the best flavour and nutrition from inexpensive cuts of meat.

Our British ancestors have taught us how to perfect the art of roasting and the traditional Sunday roast dinner is still popular with many Australian families.

In this section of the book, we have prepared traditional roasts as well as dishes for everyday use, which will enable the cook to feed the family with ease, knowing that meat includes nutrients vital to good health and well being.

Photograph opposite:
"Home on the sheep's back." Red Kelpie
mustering sheep, Wagga-Wagga,
New South Wales.

Savoury Sausage Picnic Loaf

(Photograph page 118/119)

This loaf is economical but very tasty as part of a buffet luncheon or picnic menu.

500g (1lb) sausage mince
6 shallots, chopped
2 teaspoons Angostura bitters
1 teaspoon dried mixed herbs
½ clove garlic, crushed
seasoning to taste
1 egg, beaten
1 tomato, chopped

Combine all ingredients together and form into a loaf shape. Lightly grease a meatloaf tin and spoon in the mixture pressing down well. Cover and bake at 180° (350°) for 1-1½ hours. Drain off excess fat and refrigerate. When cold serve thinly sliced.
Serves 6.

Old Fashion Meat Paste

(Photograph page 118/119)

Delicious served on hot buttered muffins or as a sandwich spread.

500g (1lb) gravy beef
½ teaspoon thyme
½ teaspoon Angostura bitters
seasoning to taste
2 onions, chopped
½ cup red wine
½ cup beef stock

Remove fat and sinew from meat and roughly chop. Combine with the other ingredients in a saucepan. Cover and simmer for 2-3 hours or until the meat is tender. Allow to cool then puree in a food processor. Transfer to a serving bowl and refrigerate.
Serves 4.

Farmhouse Paté

(Photograph page 118/119)

250g (8oz) chicken livers
2 tablespoons butter or margarine
1 onion, finely chopped
500g (1lb) minced veal
grated rind ½ lemon
1 tablespoon brandy
1 tablespoon dry white wine
½ teaspoon thyme
4 rashers bacon, rinds removed

Sauté the chicken livers in the butter with the onion. Puree in a food processor and add the remaining ingredients with the exception of the bacon. Line a small terrine with the bacon and spoon in the meat mixture. Press down firmly and cover. Cook in water bath at 180° (350°) for approximately ¾-1 hour and cool. Refrigerate untill required and serve with hot buttered toast.
Serves 6-8.

Photograph opposite:
"Bugs, Beef and Bangers" with all the goodies.
A typical "Aussie" barbeque.

Layered Chicken Paté

(Photograph page 118/119)

2 tablespoons butter or margarine
3 chicken livers, chopped
1 onion, finely chopped
250g (8oz) minced veal
250g (8oz) minced pork
1 egg, lightly beaten
1 teaspoon fresh mixed herbs, chopped
½ teaspoon freshly grated lemon rind
1 tablespoon chopped parsley
seasoning to taste
2 tablespoons dry sherry
½ cup soft wholemeal breadcrumbs
250g (8oz) chicken breasts, finely chopped

Melt the butter in a frying pan and sauté chicken livers with the onion until tender. Puree in food processor adding all the remaining ingredients with the exception of the chicken. Spoon ⅓ of the mixture into base of a greased terrine. Cover with a layer of chicken. Repeat layers ending with the chicken, and smooth over the surface. Cover and cook in a water bath at 180° (350°) for approximately 1-1½ hours. Remove from the oven, drain off excess fat and when cool refrigerate until cooled.
Serves 6.

Photograph below:
"Sheep, sheep and more sheep,"
Rosevale Sheep Station, Queensland.

Ratatouille Beef

(Photograph page 124)
Beautifully tender beef cooked in a rather attractive way with delicious fresh vegetables would make an ideal meal for a special occasion.

2kg (4lb) piece Scotch fillet
90g (3oz) butter or margarine
2 onion, sliced
1 red capsicum, sliced
1 green capsicum, sliced
2 zucchini, sliced
2 cloves garlic, crushed
¼ cup chopped parsley
½ teaspoon dried basil
seasoning to taste

Trim excess fat from fillet and slice meat at 8cm (3") intervals being careful not to slice meat right through. Melt butter in a frying pan, add prepared vegetables, herbs and seasoning, sauté gently for 3 minutes. Pack cooked vegetables into pockets of the fillet, place meat into a large roasting dish and pour over pan juices. Bake at 180° (350°) for 1¼ hours for rare beef, 1½ hours medium rare, 1¾ hours for well done.
Serves 6-8.

Beef Stroganoff

This can be made very quickly, it is beautifully flavoured, and a very suitable dish for easy entertaining.

750g (1½lb) round steak, cut into strips
seasoned flour
½ teaspoon nutmeg
60g (2oz) butter or margarine
1-2 cloves garlic, crushed
2 onions, sliced
250g (8oz) mushrooms, sliced
2 tablespoons tomato paste
¼ cup beef stock
½ cup white wine
½ cup sour cream

Toss meat in seasoned flour and nutmeg. Melt butter in a saucepan and sauté the garlic with the onions. Add the meat and brown well, then stir in the mushrooms. Combine tomato paste, stock and wine and stir into the meat. Cover and simmer approximately 20-30 munutes until meat is tender. Add sour cream, DO NOT BOIL. Serve with buttered noodles.
Serves 4.

Brawn

Brawn is usually served cold with vinegar and mustard.

500g (1lb) gravy beef roughly chopped
1 veal knuckle, cut into 3
250g (8oz) pickled pork, roughly chopped
6 peppercorns
3 cloves
½ teaspoon nutmeg
pinch herbs
1 large onion, chopped
1 carrot, chopped
1 tablespoon vinegar
2 teaspoons salt

Place meat in a large saucepan, and barely cover with water. Add remaining ingredients, cover saucepan and bring to the boil. Simmer gently for 2½-3 hours until meat is cooked and will flake easily with a fork. Drain, reserve stock and remove bones. Strain stock and return 4 cups to the saucepan. Bring to the boil and simmer for approximately 20 minutes or until stock has reduced by half. Stir into the prepared meat and vegetables. Place into a 15cm (6") x 23cm (9") wetted loaf tin or a suitable mould. Cool, then chill in refrigerator until set.

Green Peppercorn Steaks

A simple dish to make, but looks very impressive served with the peppercorn sauce.

1 clove garlic
4 thick fillet steaks
butter
½ cup orange liqueur
1 x 55g (2oz) can* green peppercorns drained
½ cup cream

Cut garlic in half and rub all over the surface of the steaks. Melt butter in a heavy based frying pan. Sear the steaks on both sides then cook as desired. Pour over the liqueur, ignite and allow the flames to die down. Remove steaks to a platter and keep warm. Stir in the peppercorns and a little extra liqueur to de-glaze the pan. Stir in the cream, adjust the seasonings if necessary, reduce heat and stir for 2-3 minutes until pan juices are blended. Spoon over steaks and serve with vegetables.
Serves 4.
*Nearest equivalent can size.

Photograph below:
Preparing for a barbeque.

Photograph opposite:
Cattle round-up, Wollogorang Station, Queensland.

Beef with Sour Cream and Mushroom Sauce

A delicately flavoured dish and will certainly impress your guests. Delicious.

4 rashers bacon, rind removed
1kg (2lb) fillet beef
2 tablespoons butter or margarine
2 onions, chopped
¼ cup carrot, chopped
¼ cup celery, chopped
seasoning to taste
1 teaspoon thyme
1 bay leaf
½ cup beef stock
¾ cup red wine

The Sauce:

pan juices
1 tablespoon butter or margarine
2 tablespoons flour
125g (4oz) button mushrooms, sliced
½ cup sour cream

Wrap the bacon around the beef and secure. Melt the butter in a roasting pan and sauté the onion with the remaining vegetables until tender. Add the beef, brown all over then add the seasonings, stock and wine. Bake at 180°C (350°F) for 1-1½ hours or until cooked. Remove from heat, keep warm. Make the sauce by bringing the pan juices to the boil. Add the combined butter and flour and cook until thickened. Add the mushrooms, gently cook for 2-3 minutes then stir in the sour cream. Reheat and serve the sauce spooned over the meat.

Mushroom and Lamb Parcels

(Photograph page 140/141)
250g (8oz) mushrooms
1 cooking apple, peeled, cored
4 sprigs mint
seasoning to taste
1.5kg (3lb) loin lamb chops, boned
butter for frying
1 packet frozen puff pastry
egg for glazing

Puree the mushrooms, apple, mint and seasoning in a food processor. Tie the chops into neat rounds and pan fry in butter for 1 minute on each side: allow to cool. Roll out pastry and cut into large squares allowing 1 square per chop, remove string and top each chop with some of the mushrooms puree. Wrap the chops in the pastry and refrigerate for 1 hour. Glaze with beaten egg and bake at 180°C (350°F) for 20-25 minutes or until cooked.
Serves 6.

Lamb in Mint Jelly

(Photograph this page)

Delicious served with a potato salad and jellied beetroot.

6 teaspoons gelatine
1½ cups hot water
2 tablespoons sugar
⅓ cup vinegar
½ cup finely chopped mint leaves
seasoning to taste
2 carrots, cooked, sliced
3-4 stuffed olives
1-2 gherkins, sliced
½ cup cooked peas
500g (1lb) cooked lamb

Dissolve the gelatine in the hot water and stir in the sugar, vinegar, mint and seasoning, allow to cool. Pour a little of the gelatine mixture into the base of a chilled wetted mould and refrigerate until the consistency of unbeaten egg white. Arrange the carrot, olives and gherkin in a decorative pattern over the jelly and refrigerate until partially set, then layer the peas alternately with the meat, seasoning well between each layer. Carefully pour in the remaining gelatine mixture and refrigerate until set. Unmould and serve with a salad.
Serves 4-6.

Seasoned Steak Roll

An interesting and tasty stuffing for this roll.

The Marinade:

½ cup olive oil
⅓ cup red wine
1 cup chopped onions
1 clove garlic, crushed
1 teaspoon oregano
½ teaspoon cayenne pepper
1 teaspoon salt
1 teaspoon black pepper

For Cooking:

1kg (2lb) piece skirt steak "butterflied"
¼ bunch silverbeet shredded
2 carrots cut into strips
2 onions sliced
2 hard-boiled eggs sliced
chopped parsley
seasoning to taste

Combine the ingredients for the marinade. Open out the meat and top with shredded silverbeet, the carrots, the onion rings and eggs. Sprinkle with chopped parsley and seasoning. Roll and tie the meat tightly and place in the marinade Refrigerate for 6 hours. Cook in the marinade until tender. Serve sliced with the cooking juices served seperately.
Serves 6.

Boeuf a la Mode

(Photograph this page)

This is a very attractive and tasty dish and needs little else but crusty bread, a green salad and a glass of wine.

1.5-2kg (5lb) topside beef
1-2 cloves garlic, slivered
2 tablespoons oil
1 onion, sliced
3 tablespoons brandy
½ cup red wine
2 pigs trotters, chopped
1 cup beef stock
3 carrots, roughly chopped
2 bay leaves
seasoning to taste
3 extra carrots, diagonally sliced

Make small incisions all over the beef and insert slivers of garlic. Heat the oil in a large saucepan and sauté the onions until tender, add the meat, turning occasionally and brown on all sides. In a smaller saucepan heat the brandy, ignite, and pour over the meat, adding the wine then simmer for 5 minutes. Transfer to a large casserole dish with the trotters and the remaining ingredients, cover and cook at 180°C (350°F) for approximately 1-1½ hours or until tender. Remove the meat from the stock and allow to cool. Strain the stock, allow to stand, then skim off any fat, re-strain, then re-boil until stock has slightly reduced, remove from heat and allow to cool. Slice the cold meat and arrange decoratively on a large platter with the extra carrots. Carefully spoon over the cold stock and garnish with fresh herbs if desired. Allow to set completely before serving.
Serves 6-8.

Veal and Peach Grill

6 large thinly sliced veal steaks
flour
60g (2oz) butter or margarine
3 peaches, peeled, sliced
1 cup ground macadamia nuts
seasoning to taste
6 slices Swiss cheese

Lightly toss the meat in the flour and melt the butter in a frying pan. Pan-fry steaks on each side until cooked. Remove from the pan and keep warm. Carefully sauté the peaches and spoon onto the veal steaks, sprinkle with macadamia nuts and season. Cover with a slice of cheese and grill until cheese melts.
Serves 6.

Lamb in Creole Sauce

2 tablespoons oil
6-8 lamb chops
4 zucchini, sliced
4 tomatoes
2 cloves garlic, crushed
1 capsicum, de-seeded, sliced
3 onions, sliced
½ teaspoon oregano
¼ teaspoon cumin
¼ teaspoon chilli powder
seasoning to taste
¼ cup red wine
2 teaspoons brown sugar
2 beef stock cubes
2 tablespoons tomato sauce
2 tablespoons flour
3 tablespoons water

Heat oil in pan, add chops and sauté both sides until browned, remove from pan. Add all prepared vegetables, oregano, cumin, chilli powder, seasoning, red wine, brown sugar, stock cubes and tomato sauce. Return meat to pan, bring to boil reduce heat, simmer covered for 30 minutes or until meat is tender.Remove meat from pan, keep warm. Mix flour and water until smooth, add to vegetable mixture stirring until sauce boils and thickens. Place chops onto serving plate. Spoon vegetable mixture over and serve with noodles or rice.
Serves 6.

Roast Lamb with Fig Sauce

(Photograph page 140/141)

An unusual but very delicious dish.

1 large leg of lamb
2 cloves garlic, slivered
1 medium onion, chopped
4 large or 6 small figs
1 cup chicken stock
½ teaspoon ground ginger
seasoning to taste

Stud the leg of lamb with the garlic. Scatter the onion over the base of a roasting dish and place the lamb on top. Roast in the usual way. Half an hour before the lamb is cooked, add the figs; remove meat from dish and keep warm. Bring pan juices to boil adding the stock, ginger and seasoning, simmer for 5 minutes. Mash the figs into the sauce which will have a lumpy appearance. Slice the lamb and serve with the accompanying sauce.
Serves 4-6.

Photograph opposite:
Saddling up, Broom Downs Station, Northern Territory.

Photograph below:
Boeuf a la Mode (Recipe this page)

Rack of Lamb and Cranberry Mousse

3 tablespoons cranberry jelly
1 tablespoon sweet fruit chutney
2 tablespoons gelatine, dissolved in water
4 egg whites
1/3 cup whipped cream
seasoning to taste
6 racks of lamb, 4 cutlets per rack

Puree the cranberry jelly, chutney and gelatine in a food processor. Pour into a glass bowl and refrigerate. Beat the egg whites stiffly, refrigerate. When the cranberry is starting to set, fold in egg whites and cream; refrigerate until set. Season lamb and bake at 200°C (400°F). Slice the lamb into single cutlets or leave in pairs and serve with the mousse.
Serves 6.

Crown Roast of Lamb

Your butcher will prepare this joint for you with reasonable notice. The roast will usually consist of twelve cutlets, sufficient for 6 people, and always looks very impressive for a dinner party.

1 crown roast
stuffing of choice (see recipes below)

Fill the cavity with chosen stuffing and place roast in baking dish. Bake at 180°C (350°F) for 1 hour.

Tipsy Sweet Potato Stuffing:

500g (1lb) sweet potato, cooked, mashed
2 tablespoons sherry
seasoning to taste
1 egg, lightly beaten
1 cup soft breadcrumbs
1 onion, finely chopped
1 tablespoon chopped parsley

Combine all ingredients together and use to stuff the meat.

Herbed Stuffing:

60g (2oz) butter or margarine
4 rashers bacon, chopped
1 onion, finely chopped
3 cups soft breadcrumbs
4 tablespoons chopped parsley
1 teaspoon marjoram
1 teaspoon thyme
1/2 teaspoon sage
seasoning to taste
1 egg, lightly beaten

Sauté bacon and onion together until onion is tender. Add breadcrumbs and herbs and when cool beat in the egg to bind ingredients together.

Photograph opposite:
"Pride of Australia", the Merino Sheep.

Photograph below:
Hahndorf, South Australia

Noisettes of Lamb and Strawberry Hollandaise

So easy to prepare and will certainly impress everyone at your next dinner party.

2 punnets strawberries
4 sprigs tarragon
2 teaspoons green peppercorns
4 egg yolks
250g (8oz) clarified butter, melted
3 tablespoons dry sherry
12-18 noisettes of lamb

Hull and wash strawberries then puree with the tarragon and peppercorns. Make the Hollandaise sauce by beating the egg yolks in the top of a double saucepan over simmering water, when very thick, remove from the heat and pour in the butter, drip by drip to start with and then faster as it combines more easily into the egg. Now beat in half to the strawberry puree and refrigerate. Stir the sherry into the remaining puree and refrigerate. Grill or pan fry the lamb to your liking. Spoon 2-3 tablespoons of the strawberry and sherry puree onto the base of warm plates and spread over evenly. Place two or three noisettes (with skewers or string removed) in the centre of the puree so they overlap and spoon over some of the strawberry Hollandaise sauce. Serve garnished with small sprigs of fennel or dill.
Serves 4-6.

Veal Pudding

500g (1lb) minced veal
60g (2oz) butter or margarine
30g (1oz) Parmesan cheese
125g tomatoes, skinned, seeded, chopped
4 eggs
seasoning, nutmeg to taste
3 leaves silver beet, shredded
1 slice wholemeal bread, soaked in milk
3 tablespoons breadcrumbs

The Sauce:

125g (4oz) tuna
4 anchovy fillets
2 teaspoons capers
2 teaspoons lime juice
seasoning to taste
1 egg yolk
¾ cup oil, approximatley

Sauté the veal in the butter until just tender, transfer to a bowl and stir in the remaining ingredients with the exception of the breadcrumbs. Pour into a well greased 4 cup mould, sprinkle with breadcrumbs and bake at 180°C (350°F) for 1 hour or until cooked. Meanwhile make the sauce by combining all the ingredients for the sauce in a blender or food processor, add sufficient oil to make a thin pouring sauce and heat gently. To serve, turn the pudding onto a serving plate and serve with the warm sauce.
Serves 3-4.

Caraway Flambe Steaks

Kummel is extracted from caraway seeds, and with the two combined, they add an unusual flavour to the veal.

125g (4oz) butter or margarine
1 onion, finely chopped
1 clove garlic, crushed
1 teaspoon caraway seeds
seasoning to taste
8 veal escalopes
½ cup Kummel liqueur
½ cup thickened cream
2 cooking apples peeled, cored, quartered

Melt half the butter in a large frying pan and add onion, garlic and caraway seeds; sauté until onion is tender. Season meat and brown on both sides. Pour in liqueur, ignite, then stir in cream. Reduce heat and stir until sauce thickens. Serve garnished with apple quarters which have been sautéed in the remaining butter.
Serves 4.

Veal and Prune Terrine

Delicious!!!

12 prunes, pitted
4 tablespoons Creme de Cacao liqueur
1 tablespoon Cognac
500g (1lb) veal mince
2 shallots, chopped
2 eggs
1 teaspoon salt
1 teaspoon pink peppercorns
4 rashers rindless bacon

Soak the prunes in the Creme de Cacao and Cognac for 24 hours before use. Combine the veal, shallots, eggs, salt and peppercorns in a bowl. Stir well. Line a 4-5 cup terrine dish with 3 rashers of bacon. Place half the veal mixture into the dish. Strain the prunes and place them down the middle of meat; cover with remaining veal. Spoon over 2 tablespoons of the Creme de Cacao mixture and top with the remaining rasher of bacon. Cook at 190°C (370°F) for 1-1½ hours, until cooked. Remove the terrine from the oven and place a weight on the top. Allow to cool then remove from the dish and refrigerate. Serve sliced, with hot toast.

Roast Veal with Paprika Sauce

Paprika Sauce:

½ cup finely chopped carrot
½ cup finely chopped celery
¼ cup finely chopped onion
1 tablespoon paprika
1 bay leaf
1 clove crushed garlic
pinch thyme
seasoning to taste
dash Worcestershire sauce
2 cups chicken stock
1 cup tomato puree

For Cooking:

2kg (4lb) boned, rolled veal
1 clove crushed garlic
seasoning to taste

Make the sauce by combining all the ingredients in a saucepan. Bring to the boil, reduce the heat and simmer for 25 minutes. Allow to cool slightly, then puree in a food processor. Place the veal on a rack in a roasting dish, rub with garlic and season. Roast at 180°C (350°F) for approximately 1¾ hours or until cooked to suit your taste. Carve and serve with reheated sauce.
Serves 6-8.

Veal and Pork Sausages

There are numerous varieties of sausages to buy these days. Try making these tasty ones yourself.

500g (1lb) minced veal
250g (8oz) minced pork
¼ teaspoon nutmeg
½ teaspoon marjoram
½ teaspoon caraway seeds
seasoning to taste
¼ cup brandy
¼ cup water
sausage casing, from your local butcher

Place all the ingredients, with the exception of the sausage casings, into a bowl and combine well together. To fill sausage cases, knot one end of the casing. Use a piping bag to fill them. Pull the open end over the nozzle and squeeze the mixture into casing. Tie into sausage lengths that suit you. Refrigerate for 1 hour before cooking.
Serves 3-4.

Photograph opposite:
"Golden" memories from the 'Good Old Days', Ballarat, Victoria.

Photograph below:
City Hall, Broken Hill, New South Wales.

Pork with Prune and Apple Stuffing

60g (2oz) butter or margarine
1 green apple, finely chopped
125g (4oz) prunes, pitted
1 onion, finely chopped
1 nob root ginger, finely chopped
6 slices stale bread, crumbed
¼ teaspoon mixed herbs
seasoning to taste
2kg (4lb) loin of pork, boned
2 teaspoons salt
¼ cup oil

Melt butter in a frying pan and sauté the apple with the prunes, onion and ginger for 3 minutes. Remove from heat and stir in breadcrumbs, herbs, seasoning. Unroll loin, skin side down, and place prepared stuffing down centre of meat. Roll up firmly and secure with string. Rub rind with salt and oil. Bake at 220°C (440°F) for 1½-2 hours or until cooked.
Serves 4-6.

Blue Vein Schnitzels

So quick and easy to prepare.

4 veal steaks
125g (4oz) butter or margarine
60g (2oz) blue vein cheese
seasoned flour
1 egg, beaten
¼ cup milk
dried breadcrumbs
¼ cup oil
60g (2oz) butter or margarine
lemon wedges

Pound veal steaks until thin. Cream butter and blue vein cheese together until smooth. Spread a little of the blue vein butter onto one side of each steak and dust with seasoned flour. Dip in combined egg and milk. Press breadcrumbs on firmly, then refrigerate for 1 hour. Melt oil and butter and sauté steaks until golden brown, turning once. Serve garnished with lemon wedges.
Serves 4.

Photograph pages 136/137:
Top right: "They're off." Racing for the 1986 Melbourne Cup (Top right).
Bottom left: Competitors returning to saddling enclosure.
Bottom right: The winner "At Talaq", in the winner's circle.

Photograph pages 138/139:
Cattle droving, Wollogorang Cattle Station, Queensland.

Photograph pages 140/141:
Top: Roast Lamb with Fig Sauce (Recipe page 129)
Bottom left: Rack of Lamb with Parsley and Sesame Seeds (Recipe page 125)
Bottom right: Mushroom and Lamb Parcels (Recipe page 120)

Photograph opposite:
Prime Ribs Piquant (Recipe page 135)

Photograph below:
Sheep droving, Canberra, Australian Capital Territory

Banana Veal Stroganoff

6 veal escalopes, flattened
seasoning to taste
½ cup chopped marjoram
½ cup parsley butter
4 bananas
3 tablespoons banana liqueur
2 eggs beaten
breadcrumbs for coating
1 cup sliced mushrooms
½ packet pre-cooked pasta
½ cup sour cream
2 tablespoons mustard

Lay the veal flat onto the work surface, season and sprinkle with the herbs. Roll up and secure, then sauté in the butter for 10 minutes until golden and cooked on both sides. Remove from the pan and keep warm. Dip the bananas in the liqueur, egg and breadcrumbs, then sauté until golden; remove from the pan and keep warm. Add a little more butter to the pan, sauté the mushrooms then add the pasta, sour cream and mustard, stir until heated through and the pasta is well coated. Arrange the veal and bananas on a serving plate and serve the pasta sauce as an accompaniment.
Serves 4.

Loin of Pork with Avocado and Apple Sauce

1.5kg (3lb) whole pork loin
seasoning to taste
½ teaspoon tarragon

The Sauce:

1 large ripe avocado, peeled, seed removed
2 small granny smith apples, peeled, cored
¼ teaspoon Tabasco sauce
½ tablespoon lemon juice
½ cup cream

For Garnish:

1 small avocado, sliced

Dust the inside of the pork with the seasoning and tarragon. Roll up and secure. Bake at 200°C (400°F) until cooked. Make the sauce by pureeing the avocado with 1 apple, a dash of Tabasco and the lemon juice. When smooth add the cream and refrigerate. Reheat carefully, just prior to serving add the remaining finely chopped apple and serve with the carved meat, garnished with slices of avocado.
Serves 6.

Prime Ribs Piquant

(Photograph this page)

1.5 kg (3lb) Rib Roast
Seasoning to taste
1 teaspoon paprika
2 cloves garlic, crushed
1¼ cups red wine
1¼ cups wine vinegar

Rub the seasonings and garlic into the meat. Marinate in the combined wine and vinegar for 4-6 hours. Roast on a rack at 180°C (350°F) allowing about 40 minutes per kg for medium to rare and serve with jacket potatoes, sour cream and horseradish sauce.

COUNTRY COOKING

No matter where you visit throughout Australia's country town communities, you will always see the skills of homemade produce shining through. Australians take great pride in sharing their tasty offerings, and recipes are often passed from one generation to the next. You can almost smell the delicious aroma of country cooking floating through the farmyard on a cold winter's morning — homemade porridge and freshly baked bread with lashings of butter and homemade jam or marmalade. Nostalgic visions of country kitchens full of bubbling pans of fruit can be transferred quite easily to small homes in the city. Summer season fruit like raspberries and strawberries are over so quickly, but by making the fruit into jam, you can capture the flavour to provide delicious all year round enjoyment.

Farmers' lunch sandwiches are spread with tasty cheese and chutneys. The results of home pickling, are invariably tastier and cheaper than shop bought varieties and you can cut costs by buying when there is a glut and prices are down.

Afternoon tea delights such as wholemeal fruit scones, nutty gingerbread, apple pies and shortbread are country inspired recipes and in this section we bring you a host of delicious country recipes which we hope you will enjoy with visiting friends.

Photograph page 142:
"Jolly Swagman, camped by the billabong."

Pineapple and Tomato Chutney

(Photograph page 147)

A sweet and spicy chutney which will accompany almost anything to add an extra touch of flavour.

1kg (2lb) pineapple, peeled, finely chopped
1.5kg (3lb) tomatoes, peeled, de-seeded, chopped
1½ cups raisins
2½ cups raw sugar
2 cups vinegar
1 green apple, peeled, cored, chopped
1½ tablespoons salt
3 tablespoons curry powder
2 teaspooon ground ginger
1 tablespoon Tabasco sauce
1 teaspoon powdered cloves

Combine all the ingredients in a large preserving pan or saucepan. Boil uncovered for 1-1½ hours or until the mixture thickens, then remove from the heat. Cool and bottle. Store in a cool place for 1 month before using.

Paw-Paw and Apple Chutney

(Photograph page 147)

Excellent served with cold meats, and makes an excellent gift for friends.

1kg (2lb) peeled, de-seeded, chopped paw paw
1 large green apple, peeled, cored, chopped
500g (1lb) onions, chopped
1¾ cups sugar
2 cups white vinegar
1 cup raisins
1 tablespoon caraway seeds
1 tablespoon ground cumin
1 teaspoon salt

Combine all ingredients in a preserving pan or heavy based saucepan. Bring to the boil, then allow to simmer until the mixture thickens, stirring occasionally to prevent the mixture catching. Pour into sterilised jars when cool, seal and store.

Quince Jelly

(Photograph page 147)

2kg (4lb) quinces
12 cups water
sugar

Wash the quince but do not peel or core. Roughly chop and place in a saucepan with ⅔ of water. Cover and simmer for 1 hour or until the fruit is tender, strain the liquid and reserve. Return the pulp to the saucepan and simmer for 30 minutes, strain combining the two liquids. Allow 500g (1lb) sugar to each 2½ cups liquid. bring the juice to the boil, stir in the sugar, bring back to the boil. Boil rapidly until setting point is obtained. Skim well and pour into small hot jars, cover, label and store.

Photograph below:
A cuddly Koala,
an Australian Heritage

Lemon Butter

125g (4oz) butter
½ cup lemon juice
2 teaspoons grated lemon rind
1½ cups sugar
2 egg yolks
4 eggs

Use a double saucepan and melt the butter over hot water. Add the lemon juice, rind and sugar. Stir until sugar has dissolved. Beat egg yolks and extra eggs until thick. Blend in a little of the hot butter mixture, then add the eggs into the hot butter, in the double saucepan. Cook, and refrigerate in a covered container. Lemon butter will keep for approximately 1 week.

Fig Jam

750g (1½lb) dessert figs, roughly chopped
1½ cups fresh orange juice
¼ cup fresh lemon juice
3½ cups sugar

Place figs, fruit juices and sugar into a large saucepan. Stir over a medium heat until sugar has dissolved. Bring to boil and continue boiling 25 minutes or until jam jells. Pour into hot sterilised jars, seal and store.

Grapefruit and Lemon Marmalade

3 grapefruits
4 lemons
8 cups water
1.5kg (3lb) sugar

Slice fruit removing seeds. Place into a large saucepan with the water. Bring to the boil, reduce heat and simmer approximately 30-40 minutes or until fruit is tender. Add the sugar and stir over a low heat until dissolved. Bring to boil approximately 45 minutes or until a jell forms. Pour into hot, sterilised jars. Seal and store.

Carrot Marmalade

1 orange halved, sliced
1 lemon halved, sliced
4 cups water
3 cups sugar
2 cups grated carrot

Place the orange and the lemon into a large saucepan with the water. Bring to the boil, reduce heat and simmer covered until fruit is tender, approximately 20 minutes. Add sugar and carrot. Stir until sugar dissolves. Bring to boil and continue boiling uncovered 45 minutes or until marmalade jells. Pour into hot, sterilised jars. Seal and store.

Citrus Marmalade

(Photograph page 147)

1 grapefruit
1 lemon
1 green apple
1 orange
4 cups water
6 cups sugar

Roughly chop unpeeled citrus fruits. Puree grapefruit and lemon in a food processor and transfer to a large saucepan. Peel quarter and core apple, finely chop in the food processor with the orange. Add to pan with water and sugar. Stir over low heat until sugar dissolves, then increase heat and boil rapidly, uncovered approximately 45 minutes or until marmalade jells. Pour into hot, sterilised jars. Seal while hot and store.

Photograph below:
Apple Strudle (Recipe page 153)

Easy Marmalade

(Photograph this page)
grated rind 1 lemon
1½ cups water
3 teaspoons gelatine
1 tablespoon lemon juice
2 tablespoons sugar

Soak lemon rind in water for 24 hours. Sprinkle over the gelatine and stir to combine. Bring to the boil, add lemon juice and sugar, and gently simmer for 10 minutes. Allow to cool, then pour into sterilised glass jar. Seal and store in the refrigerator. Will keep approximately 10 days, stored in the refrigerator.

Photograph below:
Left: Easy marmalade (Recipe this page)
Right: Carrot marmalade (Recipe page 145)

Preserved Oranges

6 firm oranges, halved
3 cups water
¼ teaspoon bicarbonate of soda
2 cups white vinegar
2 cups sugar
1 teaspoon whole cloves
2 cinnamon sticks

Slice oranges, remove seeds and place in a saucepan with water and bicarbonate of soda. Bring to boil, reduce heat, simmer 5 minutes. Drain oranges, reserving 1 cup of liquid. Place all remaining ingredients into pan with reserved liquid. Bring to boil stirring until sugar has dissolved, simmer 10 minutes. Add reserve liquid, bring back to boil. Pour syrup and oranges into hot, sterilised jars. Seal, store in a cool place. Keep 2 weeks before using.

Spicy Tomato Sauce

2kg (4lb) ripe tomatoes, halved
2 onions, quartered
1 clove garlic, crushed
1 cup white vinegar
¾ cup firmly packed brown sugar
½ teaspoon chilli powder
1 teaspoon cloves
1 teaspoon peppercorns
1 teaspoon curry powder
1 tablespoon salt
½ teaspoon allspice
1 teaspoon paprika
¼ teaspoon black pepper
pinch cayenne pepper

Finely chop the tomatoes and place into a large pan. Chop onions, add to tomatoes with garlic and vinegar. Bring to boil, reduce heat and simmer 45 minutes. Strain pulp, pressing down with the back of a spoon. Return liquid to pan discarding pulp. Add remaining ingredients to pan. Bring to boil, reduce heat and simmer until sauce has thickened approximately 30 minutes. Pour into hot, sterilised jars, seal and store.

Mustard

(Photograph this page)
Marvellous to serve with cold meats, and so easy to make.

150g (5oz) dry mustard seeds
1 medium onion, chopped
2 cloves garlic, crushed
1 teaspoon salt
2 teaspoons ground black pepper
1 bay leaf
2 teaspoons Tabasco sauce
2 tablespoons golden syrup
1 tablespoon curry powder
1 cup white wine
1 chicken stock cube

Combine all the ingredients in a saucepan and cover with water. Leave to soak for 1 hour, drain and add fresh water to cover. Leave for 2 hours then simmer for the next hour, stirring frequently to prevent the mixture catching, adding more water or wine as required. Remove from the heat and cool. Place in a processor or blender and roughly chop but do not puree. Pour into sterilised bottles or jars and store in cool place for 1 week.

Pickled Beetroot

Delicious served with salads and cold meats.

4 beetroot
1½ cups white vinegar
¾ cup water
¾ cup sugar
½ teaspoon peppercorns
½ teaspoon cloves
1 bay leaf
½ teaspoon mustard seeds
½ cinnamon stick
¼ teaspoon salt

Wash beetroot well, cook in boiling, salted water until tender. Cool, and remove skins, either peeling by hand for a smooth surface or with a knife. If beetroot are large, cut in half, then slice into julienne strips. Place vinegar, water, sugar, peppercorns, cloves, bay leaf, mustard seeds, cinnamon stick and salt into pan, bring to boil. Simmer 5 minutes and strain. Spoon beetroot into hot, sterilised jars and top up with the vinegar mixture. Seal. Store in a cool place.

Capsicum Pickle

6 red capsicum
6 green capsicuim
6 cups tarragon or white wine vinegar
1 teaspoon salt
1 tablespoon sugar
sprigs fresh tarragon
1 small onion
1 small tablespoon black peppercorns

Wash capsicums, slice in half lengthwise, removing seeds and cores, cut into thin strips. Arrange capsicums in layers of colour in hot sterilised jars. Bring vinegar, salt and sugar to boil, pour over capsicums and decorate pickle with sprigs of fresh tarragon oinon rings and peppercorns. Seal and store.

Photograph below:
Top left: Pineapple and Tomato Chutney (Recipe page 144)
Top middle: Spicy Tomato Sauce (Recipe page 146)
Top right: Paw Paw and Apple Chutney (Recipe page 144)
Centre right: Quince Jelly (Recipe page 144)
Front left: Citrus Marmalade (Recipe page 145)
Front right: Mustard (Recipe this page)

Honey Peach Jam

1kg (2lb) peaches
½ cup water
1½ cups sugar
½ cup honey

Peel, halve, stone, and slice peaches and place in a saucepan with water, sugar and honey. Stir over a low heat until sugar dissolves. Bring to boil and continue boiling 45 minutes or until jam jells. Pour into hot, sterilised jars. Seal and store.

Damper

2 cups self-raising flour
½ teaspoon salt
1¼ cups milk, approximately

Sift the flour and salt into a bowl, add sufficient milk to make a manageable dough. Bake on greased and floured baking sheet 25-30 minutes at 220°C (440°F). Baste with milk during cooking. Serve with lashings of butter.

Crunchy Muffins

125g (4oz) butter or margarine
¾ cup brown sugar
grated rind ½ orange
1 egg, beaten
1 cup cereal, crushed
½-¾ cup milk
1½ cups self-raising flour, sifted
¼ teaspoon salt

Topping:

½ cup brown sugar
½ cup pecan nuts, chopped
½ teaspoon cinnamon

Cream the butter and sugar together with the grated orange rind. Add the egg gradually, then the cereal. Add the milk alternately with the flour and salt and divide the mixture equally between 16 greased muffin or deep patty tins. Combine the ingredients for the topping and sprinkle over the muffins. Bake at 190°C (370°F) for 15-20 minutes. Serve warm.
Makes 16 muffins.

Banana and Passionfruit Butter

This makes an excellent cake filling, or spread for scones.

2 medium bananas, peeled
2 passionfruit
grated rind and juice 2 lemons
250g (8oz) butter
⅓ cup sugar
¼ teaspoon salt
2 egg yolks, beaten
¼ cup orange liqueur

Mash the bananas. Halve the passionfruit and scoop out the pulp. Place all the ingredients into the top of a double saucepan and cook over a medium heat, stirring or whisking until thickened. Bottle in sterilised jars and seal.

Photograph opposite:
Left: Mandarin and Apple Flan.
Right: Caramel Cremes.

Photograph below:
"A Country Kitchen," Queensland.

Caramel Cremes

(Photograph this page)

90g (3oz) caster sugar
½ cup water
2¼ cups milk
30g (1oz) sugar
¼ teaspoon vanilla essence
2 eggs, beaten
2 egg yolks

Dissolve sugar in the water and bring to the boil without stirring until a rich brown colour is achieved. Pour immediately into dry, hot individual moulds, allow to coat the base and sides, leave to cool. Heat the milk and sugar with the vanilla and pour onto the beaten eggs. Cool and strain. Pour into the prepared moulds, cover with greasproof paper or foil and cook in a water bath at 180°C for 25-30 minutes or until firm. Leave to cool, then serve, with chocolate coated strawberries.
Serves 4.

Mixed Fruit Wholemeal Scones

The name tells the story, your taste buds do the rest.

1½ cups wholemeal self-raising flour
½ cup self-raising flour
¼ teaspoon salt
30g (1oz) butter or margarine
¾ cup mixed fruit
2 tablespoons brown sugar
¾-1 cup milk

Sift the flour and salt together. Rub the butter into the flour and stir in the mixed fruit and sugar. Mix to a soft dough with the milk. Turn onto a floured board and light knead until smooth and elastic. Roll or press out to 2cm (¾") thickness. Cut into shape; using a 6cm (2½") fluted scone cutter. Place on baking sheet and glaze with milk. Bake at 220°C (440°F) for 10-15 minutes or until cooked. Serve warm with butter or margarine.
Makes 10-12 scones.

Mandarin and Apple Flan

(Photograph this page)

1 quantity sweet shortcrust pastry
1 cup custard
2 apples, cored, thinly sliced
2 canned peach halves, drained
2 x 312g (10oz) cans* mandarin segments, drained
4 tablespoons apricot jam

Line a 30cm (12") flan tin with pastry and bake blind at 190°C (370°F) for 15-20 minutes. Allow to cool, spoon the custard into the base of the flan. Arrange fruit over the top and sprinkle with lemon juice. Heat the jam in a small saucepan, and gently brush over the fruit. Allow to cool before slicing.
Serves 8-10.

*Nearest equivalent can size

Spiced Apple Cake

(Photograph page 156)
Delicious served warm with
fresh cream.
The Topping:
2 tablespoons brown sugar
½ teaspoon cinnamon
½ teaspoon nutmeg
3 tablespoons flour
15g (¾oz) melted butter or margarine
The Cake:
¾ cup milk
1 cup muesli
1 egg, beaten
⅓ cup brown sugar
60g (2oz) melted butter or margarine
1 cup peeled, grated apple
1¾ cups self-raising flour
1 teaspoon baking powder
½ teaspoon cinnamon
½ teaspoon nutmeg

Mix dry topping ingredients together
and stir in the butter. Combine the
milk and muesli and stand for 5
minutes, then add the egg. Add
sugar, butter and apple, then fold in
the sifted dry ingredients. Pour into
a prepared 20cm (8″) springform tin.
Crumble the topping over the cake
mixture. Bake at 180°C (350°F) for 30-
35 minutes. Allow cake to stand 15-20
minutes before turning out. Eat
within 2-3 days.
Makes 1 cake.

Bran Scones

Healthy wholemeal bran scones.
*3 cups wholemeal self-raising flour,
sifted*
1 cup bran
2 tablespoons brown sugar
½ cup dates, chopped
1 teaspoon mixed spice
60g (2oz) butter or margarine
2 tablespoons honey
1-1½ cups milk

Place the flour, bran, brown sugar,
dates and spice into a bowl. Melt
the butter and honey in the milk and
stir into the dry ingredients. Turn
onto a floured board and knead
lightly, cut out scones using 6cm
(2½″) scone cutter. Place on a
baking sheet. Brush with milk and
bake at 220°C (440°F) for 12-14
minutes or until golden.
Makes 18 scones.

Date and Walnut Roll

1½ cups chopped dates
60g (2oz) butter or margarine
1 cup brown sugar
1 cup water
½ teaspoon bicarbonate of soda
1 egg, lightly beaten
½ cup chopped walnuts
2 cups self-raising flour, sifted

Combine dates, butter, brown sugar
and water in a saucepan and stir
over low heat until the sugar has
dissolved. Bring to the boil, remove
from heat and allow to cool. Stir in
the bicarbonate of soda, egg and
walnuts, then add the flour. Spoon
mixture into two greased nut roll tins
and bake at 180°C (350°F) for 40-45
minutes.
Makes 2 rolls.

Photograph opposite:
A Country Homestead, Queensland.

Photograph pages 154/155:
Sour Cherry Chicken (Recipe page 166)

Photograph below:
Conargo Junction, New South Wales.

Prune and Apple Dessert Cake

(Photograph page 156)

The Topping:

¼ cup walnuts, chopped
10 prunes
1 apple, peeled, cored, sliced

The Base:

125g (4oz) butter or margarine
⅓ cup brown sugar
½ cup honey
2 eggs, beaten
1 cup cereal, finely crushed
2 cups self-raising flour or wholemeal
self-raising flour
½ teaspoon salt
½ teaspoon mixed spice
½ teaspoon nutmeg
⅔-¾ cup water

Grease and flour a 20cm (8″) springform tin. Decorate base, using the topping ingredients. Make the base by creaming the butter, sugar and honey together unti light and fluffy. Gradually add the beaten eggs, alternately with the cereal. Sift the flour, salt and spices together and add to the creamed mixture alternately with the water and spoon into the prepared tin. Bake at 180°C (350°F) for 45-50 minutes or until cooked.
Serves 6.

Apricot Brazil Ring Cake

½ cup chopped dates
¼ cup chopped dried apricots
1 cup muesli
1 cup boiling water
125g (4oz) butter or margarine
¾ cup caster sugar
2 eggs, beaten
2 cups self-raising flour
½ teaspoon mixed spice
⅓ cup brazil nuts, chopped
lemon icing
extra chopped or whole dried apricots
flaked brazil nuts

Soften dates, apricots and muesli in a bowl with the water for 15 minutes. Cream butter and sugar together until light and fluffy then gradually add the eggs. Stir in the fruits, muesli, flour, spice and brazil nuts. Spoon into a 20cm (8″) ring tin and bake at 180°C (350°F) for 45-55 minutes, or until cooked. Allow to cool in the tin before turning out. Ice whilst warm, and decorate with apricots and brazil nuts.
Makes 1 cake.

Photograph below:
"Sages Cottage" Baxter, Victoria.

Chocolate and Fruit Cake

½ cup raisins
¼ cup rum
3 cups self-raising flour
¼ teaspoon salt
1 teaspoon bicarbonate of soda
185g (6oz) butter or margarine
1¼ cups caster sugar
3 eggs
1½ cups milk
100g (3½oz) cooking chocolate,
melted, cooled

Soak the raisins in the rum for at least 2 hours. Grease and line 3 x 20cm (8″) sandwich tins with greaseproof paper. Sift the flour, salt and bicarbonate of soda together. Cream the butter and sugar together, add the eggs one at a time, beating well after each addition, then add the milk, chocolate and strained rum alternately with the flour mixture, beat well. Pour the mixture into the tins and bake at 200°C (400°F) for 30-40 minutes. Allow to cool, then serve the cakes plain, with icing cream or with a chocolate frosting.

Photograph and recipe opposite:
Apple Pie

Apple Pie

(Photograph this page)

Always a family favourite
8 large green apples
¼ cup sugar
½ cup water
¼ teaspoon cinnamon
⅓ cup sultanas
185g (6oz) butter or margarine, cubed
½ cup sugar
1 egg separated
1½ cups flour
¾ cup self-raising flour
⅓ cup cornflour
½ cup milk approximately, for glazing
extra sugar
extra cinnamon

Peel, quarter, core and slice apples
and place in a large saucepan with
the sugar, water and cinnamon.
Bring to the boil, reduce heat and
simmer, covered 8 minutes, or until
apples are tender but still holding
their shape. Drain apples if any
liquid remains and stir in the
sultanas. Cool. Cream the butter and
sugar together, then beat in the egg
yolk. Add the dry ingredients and
knead into a dough. Roll out ⅔ of
pastry and use to line base and sides
of greased 20cm (8″) springform
tin and spread the apple mixture
evenly over base. Roll out remaining
pastry, to cover the pie. Seal edges
together and trim. Brush top with
the lightly beaten egg white, sprinkle
with the extra sugar and cinnamon.
Cut 2 slits in the top. Bake at 180°C
(350°F) for 15 minutes, reduce heat to
150°C (300°F), cook a further 35
minutes, or until pie is golden brown
and pastry is cooked. Serve hot or
cold with cinnamon cream, or ice
cream.
Serves 8-10.

Delicious Date Cake

3/4 cup evaporated milk, scalded
1 cup chopped dates
125g (4oz) butter or margarine
1/2 cup caster sugar
1 egg lightly beaten
1 cup self-raising flour
1/2 cup chopped walnuts
1 tablespoon butter or margarine, melted, optional
3 teaspoons cinnamon sugar, optional

Pour the milk over the dates and leave to cool. Cream the butter and sugar in a bowl then add the egg and beat well to combine. Fold in the flour, mixing alternatively with the milk and dates, finally add the walnuts. Place the mixture into a greased 20cm (8") ring tin and bake at 180°C (350°F) for 45 minutes approximately. Brush with a little butter and cinnamon sugar if desired.

Jam Fingers

3 cups flour
1 teaspoon baking powder
250g (8oz) butter or margarine
1 cup caster sugar
1 egg, lightly beaten
2 teaspoons vanilla essence
1 cup raspberry jam, warmed

Sift the flour and baking powder into a bowl then rub in the butter and stir in the sugar. Add the egg and vanilla essence and mix to a stiff dough. Knead lightly. Press 2/3rds of dough into a greased and lined lamington tin, spread with the jam. Roll out the remaining dough and cut into 1 cm (1/2") strips. Decorate the top in the form of a lattice pattern and bake at 180°C (350°F) for 40 minutes approximately. Cool in the tin and cut into small squares to serve.

Coconut Lemon Slice

250g (8oz) coffee biscuits, crushed
grated rind 2 lemons
1 cup dessicated coconut
1/2 cup condensed milk
125g (4oz) butter or margarine

Combine the biscuits, rind and coconut in a bowl, mix well, set aside. Gently heat the condensed milk and butter in a saucepan until mixture has melted then pour over the dry ingredients. Mix well and place the mixture into a greased lamington tin, refrigerate until set then ice with lemon icing and cut into small squares.

Photograph page opposite:
Shearing at Glenisla Station, Victoria.

Photograph below:
Pork and Veal Pie (Recipe page 167)

Fruit and Nut Bars

(Photograph page 163)
2 eggs
¾ cup caster sugar
4 cups Rice Bubbles, crushed
1 teaspoon baking powder
1 cup pitted dates, coarsely chopped
1 cup mixed nuts
⅓ dried peaches, chopped

Beat the eggs until light and fluffy, then gradually add the sugar, beating until the mixture thickens. Combine with the Rice Bubbles, baking powder, dates, nuts and peaches. Press into a greased 23cm (9″) x 23cm (9″) slab tin and bake at 180°C (350°F) for 20-25 minutes. Mark into bars before allowing to cool.
Makes approximately 32.

Pecan Weet-Bix Cookies

(Photograph page 163)
125g (4oz) butter or margarine
½ cup sugar
1 egg
1 cup flour
3 tablespoons cornflour
6 Weet-Bix crushed
1 teaspoon baking powder
pecan halves

Cream the butter and sugar together until light and fluffy, then add all the dry ingredients with the exception of the pecans. Roll into balls and place on greased baking sheets, pressing a pecan into the center of each cookie. Bake at 180°C (350°F) for approximately 15 minutes.
Makes approximately 32.

Chocolate Afghans

(Photograph page 163)
Afghans are a favourite with most Australians and so it was a must to include them in this section.
220g (7oz) butter or margarine
90g (3oz) caster sugar
185g (6oz) flour, sifted
1 tablespoon cocoa, sifted
2½ cups crushed Weet-Bix
chocolate icing, optional

Cream the butter and sugar until light and fluffy. Add dry ingredients and place teaspoons of mixture onto greased baking sheets pressing down slightly with a fork. Bake at 180°C (350°F) for 12-15 minutes, and ice when cold if wished.
Makes approximately 30.

Raisin Orange Gems

(Photograph page 163)
A tasty treat for afternoon tea.
3 cups cornflakes
1¼ cups self-raising flour, sifted
155g (5oz) butter or margarine
½ cup brown sugar
1 egg
1 teaspoon grated orange rind
1 cup coconut
⅓ cup glacé cherries, chopped
¾ cup raisins, halved

Crush cornflakes finely and combine with the flour. Cream the butter and sugar together until light and fluffy then beat in the egg. Add the orange rind, coconut, cherries and raisins, and combine with dry ingredients. Place heaped teaspoons of mixture onto greased baking sheets and bake at 180°C (350°F) for 10-15 minutes. Cool before storing.
Makes approximately 32.

Chocolate Puffed Wheat Crisps

(Photograph page 163)
These crisps are best eaten the day they are made.
185g (6oz) butter or margarine
185g (6oz) caster sugar
1 egg beaten
2 cups self-raising flour, sifted
1 tablespoon cocoa, sifted
⅓ cup walnuts, finely chopped
½ cup puffed wheat

Cream the butter and sugar until light and fluffy then beat in the egg. Combine the flour and cocoa, stir into the creamed mixture together with the walnuts and puffed wheat. Place heaped tablespoons of mixture onto greased baking sheets. Bake at 180°C (350°F) for 12-15 minutes. Cool, for a minute before transferring to a cooling rack.
Makes approximately 40.

Photograph:
Top basket: Chocolate Afghans,
Fruit and Nut Bars.
Right basket: Butter Cookies.
Left basket: Chocolate Puffed Wheat Crisps,
Raisin Orange Gems.
Bottom basket: Pecan Weet-bix Cookies.

Sour Cherry Chicken

(Photograph page 154/155)

A rather delicious meal, and very colourful iwth the addition of the cherry sauce.

8 chicken breasts
dark soy sauce
8 thin slices lemon
freshly ground black pepper

Brush the chicken with soy sauce. Place a slice of lemon on each breast and season with pepper. Line a grill pan with foil and grill chicken until tender and serve with the sour cherry sauce.

Sour Cherry Sauce:

2 tablespoons cider Vinegar
4 tablespoons soft brown sugar
2 tablespoons cornflour
1 x 425g (14oz) can* black cherries pitted, drained, juice reserved
1 cup chicken stock
1 tablespoon grated orange rind
1 tablespoon grated lemon rind
½ cup orange juice
2 tablespoons lemon juice

Place vinegar and sugar in a saucepan, bring to the boil, and cook stirring constantly until mixture caramelizes. Blend cornflour with 2 tablespoons of cherry liquid, and place the remainder in a saucepan with the stock, rinds, juices, cherries and liquid, cook for a further 3 minutes. Add cornflour paste, stirring thoroughly until combined. Stir until sauce thickens.
Serves 8.
*Nearest equivalent can size.

Pheasant Braised in Brandy and Port

(Photograph page 172/173)

The fruity flavour of the port and brandy, really penetrates through the pheasant making a very tasty dish.

1kg (2lb) pheasant
flour
30g (1oz) butter or margarine
2 tablespoons oil
2 rashers bacon, chopped
1 large onion, chopped
60g (2oz) button mushrooms
4 tablespoons brandy
4 tablespoons port
2 tablespoons flour
1 cup water
seasoning to taste
1 teaspoon fresh thyme

Lightly toss pheasant in flour. Heat butter and oil in a frying pan, and brown the pheasant all over. Transfer to a casserole. Sauté the bacon, onion and mushrooms in the frying pan until golden, then add ½ the brandy and port. Simmer for 2-3 minutes, then stir in the flour and allow to brown. Whisk in the water, seasoning and thyme. Pour over pheasant, cover tightly and bake at 180°C (350°F) for 1½-2 hours adding the remaining port and brandy, ½ hour before serving.
Serves 4.

Photograph page opposite:
Sunset through the trees, Victoria.

Photograph below:
Breakfast Pie (Recipe this page)

Breakfast Pie

(Photograph this page)

A hearty country breakfast, incorporating the natural taste of cream and cheese.

2-3 tablespoons oil
2 cups uncooked potatoes, cubed
1 onion, finely chopped
220g (7oz) chopped ham
2 sticks celery, finely sliced
6 eggs, beaten
pinch thyme
¼ cup cream
½ cup grated cheese
freshly chopped parsley

Heat oil in a large frying pan and sauté the potatoes and onion for approximately 15-20 minutes. Stir frequently until they are cooked. Reduce heat and stir in the ham and celery. Combine the eggs, thyme, and cream together and pour over the potatoes. Cover and cook until the eggs are almost set, approximately 8-10 minutes. Sprinkle with the cheese, allow to melt, then serve.
Serves 4-6.

Photograph page 162:
Rodeo, Bourke, New South Wales.

Photograph page 164/165
Tomato Picking Shepparton, Victoria.

Photograph pages 168/169:
Govetts Leap, Blue Mountains, New South Wales.

Photograph pages 170/171:
Wilberforce, New South Wales.

Photograph pages 172/173:
Pheasant Braised in Brandy and Port
(Recipe page 166)

Pork and Veal Pie

(Photograph page 161)

You require: Loaf Tin 13cm × 22cm × 7.5cm (5¼in × 8½in × 3in).

Filling:

450g (1lb) Pork pieces
450g (1lb) Veal Steak, cubed
3 teaspoons gelatine
3 hard boiled eggs
1 teaspoons salt
½ teaspoon pepper
2 small onions, finely chopped
1 teaspoon mixed herbs

Pastry:

400g (3½ cups) plain flour
½ teaspoon salt
115g (4oz) lard
250ml (1 cup) milk

Place pork, veal, herbs, salt, pepper and onion into a saucepan, cover with water and simmer until meat is tender. Remove from heat set aside and allow to cool.

Preparing Pastry:

Sift flour and salt into a bowl. Place lard and milk into a saucepan and bring to the boil. Make a well in the flour and pour in boiling milk mixture. Beat thoroughly until pastry mixture leaves the sides of the bowl.

Preparing the Pie:

Take ⅔ of the pastry and roll out (on floured bench) to 1.2 cm (½in) thickness. Grease and flour the base and sides of the tin and press in pastry so that it slightly overlaps the edge. Place the hard boiled eggs into the tin and spoon in the cooled meat, setting aside the stock.
Roll out the remaining pastry and place it over the pie, trimming off the edges. Carefully pinch the sides so as to seal pie and make a small hole in the centre of pie top. Lightly brush top with milk and bake at 190°C (375°F) for 30 minutes or until golden brown. Remove from oven and allow to cool for 15 minutes. Heat 1 cup of reserved meat stock and dissolve gelatine in this. Using a funnel, very carefully pour the gelatine solution into the pie. Refrigerate for 5-6 hours. Serve cut into slices with fresh garden salads.
Serves 6-8.

GOLDEN GRAINS

Australia has abundant resources of nutritious grain-wheat, corn, rice, barley, oats — to name a few. Grains are such an important factor in the supply of fibre, essential for good health.

Few things are more satisfying to eat than homemade bread — warm and fresh from the oven, with lashings of creamy butter. There is certainly a great sense of achievement when you have produced your oven bread. Australians have shown an increasing interest in making their own bread and are finding it a challenge as well as being good fun.

We are privileged to have such a wonderful range of breads in Australia to choose. Our cosmopolitan community has influenced our desire to sample breads such as rye, black bread, pita, wholemeal and milk bread.

Our traditional bush bread — Damper — is quick and simple to make and is a great favourite. Australians love sandwiches for packed lunches and probably have at least one sandwich during the course of each day. Oats and corn are favourites as breakfast cereals and add a wonderful texture to biscuits, cakes and soups.

The following recipes supply the fibre and protein so necessary for good nutrition.

Photograph opposite:
"Golden Grains" make a wonderful
range of Golden Breads.

Health Bran Porridge

(Photograph this page)

A quick and easy breakfast for winter accompanied with fruit.

½ cup bran
½ cup rolled oats
1¾ cups hot water
milk
honey
1 tablespoon dried fruit
1 banana sliced

Combine bran, oats and water in a saucepan, bring to the boil. Simmer 5 minutes adding extra water if necessary. Sweeten to taste with honey and serve with milk, sprinkled with dried fruits and banana. Serves 4-5.

Warm-Up Porridge

(Photograph this page)

For variety, add dried fruits with the oats before cooking.

1 cup rolled oats
2½-3 cups hot water
cream or milk
honey

Place oats and water in a saucepan, bring to the boil stirring constantly, cook until soft. For extra creaminess, use milk instead of water and add extra water or milk if the porridge becomes too thick. Serve hot with milk or cream. Add honey if desired. Serves 4.

Scotch Oatmeal

5 cups cold water
2 teaspoons salt
250g (8oz) coarse oatmeal

Combine water and salt in a medium size saucepan. When almost boiling sprinkle in oatmeal, stirring continuously. Simmer 10-15 minutes. Cover and let stand for 4-5 hours or overnight. Gently re-heat when required.
Serves 4-6.

Corn Fritters

The food processor or blender will make quick work of the preparation.

2 cups canned corn kernels
seasoning to taste
1 egg
1 teaspoon oil
½ cup milk
2 cups flour
2 teaspoons baking powder
oil for frying

Puree the corn in a blender or food processor, season then add the egg, oil, milk, flour and baking powder. Heat oil in a deep fat fryer and cook tablespoons of the mixture until golden brown and cooked through. Drain and serve.
Serves 6.

Oatmeal Rolls

250g (8oz) rolled oats
2 cups milk
15g (½oz) compressed yeast
¼ cup warm water
60g (2oz) butter, melted
1 teaspoon salt
2 cups flour
egg and milk, for glazing

Place rolled oats into a bowl, pour on the milk and leave to soak for at least 2 hours. Dissolve the yeast in warm water and add this to the oats. Add the melted butter, salt and enough flour to make a smooth dough. Knead thoroughly for about 10 minutes. Replace in the bowl, cover with a cloth and leave to rise for 1 hour. Break down the dough and knead again. Shape into rolls and mark an X on the top with a sharp knife. Place on a greased baking sheet and leave to double in size. Brush with beaten egg and milk and bake at 200°C (400°F) for 15-20 minutes or until golden brown.
Makes 12 rolls.

Photograph below:
Wheat ready for harvesting
Moree, New South Wales

Potato Cakes

These are delicious served for breakfast, but just as nice served with a crisp salad.

125g (4oz) flour
½ teaspoon baking powder
½ teaspoon salt
½ teaspoon pepper
30g (1oz) butter or margarine
250g (8oz) mashed potatoes
enough milk to moisten
butter for frying

Sift flour, baking powder and salt into a bowl. Add pepper then rub in butter with finger tips as for scones. Make sure that the potatoes are very finely beaten, blend in with enough milk to make a stiff dough. Turn on to a lightly floured board, roll out to about 5mm (¼") thick, cut into rounds about 5cm (2") in diameter. Pan fry in butter until golden brown on both sides, approximately three minutes each side and serve garnished with parsley.
Makes approximately 6-8.

Photograph opposite:
"Big Red Kangaroo" and Baby Joey in pouch.

Photograph left:
Sunflower in bloom.

Photograph opposite page:
Harvesting, Willowtree, Liverpool Plains,
New South Wales.

Photograph page 184:
"Devils Marbles" near Ayres Rock,
Northern Territory.

Photograph page 186/187:
Left: Wholemeal Pasties (Recipe page 188)
Right: Cheese and Leek Quiche (Recipe page 185)

Muesli Bread

A very nicely textured healthy loaf,
which can be served fresh or
toasted, with a hot drink.

30g (1oz) compressed yeast
½ cup warm water
2 teaspoons sugar
½ cup rolled oats
½ cup dried apricots, finely chopped
2 tablespoons brown sugar
2 teaspoons salt
1 tablespoon oil
2 cups boiling water
1 egg, lightly beaten
2 cups wheatgerm
2 tablespoons skim milk powder
3 cups wholemeal flour
½ cup gluten flour
2 tablespoons soya flour
1 cup flour
extra flour for kneading

Mix the yeast in the water and stir in
the sugar until dissolved. Leave to
stand in a warm place until frothy,
about 10-20 minutes. Place the
rolled oats, apricots, sugar, salt and
oil in a large bowl. Pour the boiling
water over these ingredients and
allow to cool to lukewarm. Add the
yeast, egg, wheatgerm and
powdered milk to the lukewarm
rolled oat mixture. Mix well. Sift the
flours together and stir into the
mixture. Place 1 cup extra flour onto
a board and knead the dough for 10
minutes adding more flour if
necessary. Place in a greased bowl,
cover and allow to rise in a warm
place until double in size, about 45-
60 minutes. Punch down and form
into loaves or buns. Place in greased
tins or on greased trays and allow to
rise in a warm place for 30-45
minutes or until well rounded and
almost double in size. Bake at 200°C
(400°F) for 10 minutes, then at 180°C
(350°F) for a further 40 minutes. Brush
with butter and cool on a wire rack.
Makes 2-3 small loaves.

Raisin bread

4 cups flour
2 teaspoons salt
1 teaspoon cinnamon
1 teaspoon mixed spice
⅓ cup sugar
30g (1oz) butter or margarine
1¼ cups milk
30g (1oz) compressed yeast
1 cup raisins
milk for glazing

Sift flour, salt, cinnamon, mixed
spice and sugar together into a bowl,
and rub in butter. Heat milk to
lukewarm, add the yeast and stir
until combined. Allow to cool and
stir in sufficient liquid to make a soft
manageable dough. Knead on a
floured board and place in a lightly-
oiled bowl. Cover with a piece of
plastic wrap and a tea towel. Stand
in a warm place until dough doubles
in size, approximately 30 minutes.
Re-knead on a floured board adding
the raisins and place in a greased
28cm (11") x 12cm (5") loaf tin. Cover
and leave to prove in a warm place
until dough doubles in size,
approximately 30 minutes. Brush
lightly with milk and bake at 230°C
(450°F) for 35 minutes or
until cooked.
Makes 1 large loaf.

Wholemeal Bread

30g (1oz) compressed yeast
2 teaspoons sugar
3-3½ cups warm water
7 cups wholemeal flour
¾ cup gluten flour
2 tablespoons soya flour
3 teaspoons salt
2 tablespoons skim milk powder
3 tablespoons oil
2 teaspoons sesame seeds

Combine yeast, sugar and 2 cups of
the warm water in a warm bowl.
Cover and stand in a warm place
until the yeast froths, about 10
minutes. Sift flours, salt and milk
powder together. Add oil to the
yeast mixture with the rest of the
warm water. Pour over the dry
ingredients and mix to a soft dough.
Turn out onto a floured board and
knead until the dough is smooth,
approximately 10 minutes. Place in
an oiled basin, cover and leave in a
warm place until dough has doubled
its size. Punch down, divide the
dough and form into loaves or buns.
Place in greased bread tins or on
greased trays. Cover and allow to
rise in a warm place for 30-40
minutes. Glaze with milk, sprinkle
with sesame seeds and bake at
220°C (425°F) for 25-30 minutes or
until cooked.
Makes 3 small loaves.

Chicken and Corn Soup

A very hearty soup, filled with lots of chicken and corn, almost a meal in itself.

1 x No. 13 chicken
10 cups water
½ cup water chestnuts, drained, chopped
1 small onion, roughly chopped
2 rashers bacon, roughly chopped
1 nob root ginger, finely chopped
6 shallots, chopped
1 x 440g (14oz) can* corn nibblets
3 tablespoons cornflour
⅓ cup water
1 tablespoon sweet sherry
2 teaspoons soy sauce
1 egg
*Nearest equivalent can size.

Place chicken into a large saucepan with the water. Bring to the boil and simmer for approximately 40 minutes or until chicken is cooked. Remove chicken from pan, allow to cool, reserving stock. Remove skin and bones from chicken, chop the flesh. Add all prepared ingredients to the reserved chicken stock together with the corn niblets. Bring to the boil. Mix cornflour and water to a smooth paste, add to soup, simmer, stirring 3 minutes. Add sherry and soy sauce. Lightly beat egg with a fork, and stir into the soup. Serve at once.
Serves 10-12.

Waist-Line Luncheon

(Photograph page 185)
A quick luncheon dish for those watching their "waist".
2 hard-boiled eggs
2 slices Cheddar cheese
lettuce leaves
1 slice wholemeal bread buttered
2 sticks celery
6 dried apricots
Cut eggs in half and sandwich together with a slice of cheese. Arrange lettuce leaves over the slice of wholemeal bread and top with the celery. Serve with the eggs and apricots.
Serves 1.

Cracked Wheat and Parsley Salad

⅔ cup steamed, cracked wheat
1½ cups parsley, chopped
¾ cup mint leaves, chopped
1 clove garlic, crushed
3 tomatoes, chopped
1 onion, chopped
¼ cup olive oil
¼ cup lemon juice
seasoning to taste
Combine all the ingredients together in a large bowl and serve spooned into wholemeal pita bread.
Serves 8.

Open Soya Bean Sandwiches

Why not serve this healthy filling with one of your favourite breads.

1 x 430g (14oz) can* soya beans
1 Weet-Bix, crushed
1 cup finely chopped celery
1 cup carrot, grated
2 onions, finely chopped
½ cup grated cheese
2 eggs, beaten
½ teaspoon basil
finely chopped parsley
salt to taste
⅓ cup gluten flour
slices of rye bread
butter or margarine
lettuce leaves
*Nearest equivalent can size.

Mash soya beans and combine with the Weet-Bix, vegetables, cheese, egg and seasoning. Mix in the flour. Press into a greased 30cm (12") x 10cm (4") loaf tin and bake at 190°C (375°) for 1½ hours. Allow to cool, then refrigerate. Spread bread with butter, top with lettuce then a slice of the loaf.
Makes 1 loaf.

Basic Wholemeal Pastry

The pastry with 100's of uses. For a softer pastry use a mixture of wholemeal and plain flour.

2 cups wholemeal flour
¼-½ teaspoon salt
125g (4oz) butter or margarine
½-⅔ cup cold water

Sift dry ingredients together in a bowl and rub in the butter until mixture resembles breadcrumbs. Mix in sufficient water to make a firm but slightly moist dough. Turn out onto a floured surface, knead slightly and roll out to required size. Makes 1 x 30cm (12″) pie base.

Tasty Cheese and Leek Quiche

(Photograph page 187)
An excellent light luncheon or entree, which can be served either warm or cold, with a crisp salad.

1 quantity wholemeal pastry (refer Basic Wholemeal Pastry recipe)
2 tablespoons oil
1 leek, washed, finely sliced
1 cup button mushrooms, finely sliced
4 eggs, beaten
1½ cups milk
1 cup cream
1 tablespoon cornflour
¾ cup grated cheese
freshly ground nutmeg

Line a deep 23cm (9″) quiche tin or a shallow 30cm (12″) flan tin with the thinly rolled pastry and refrigerate for 30 minutes. Heat the oil in a frying pan and sauté the leeks for 3-4 minutes. Add mushrooms and cook 1 minute. Combine eggs, milk and mix with the cornflour, whisk into the egg mixture. Spread leeks and mushrooms over the base of the quiche, sprinkle with cheese and nutmeg and bake at 190°C (375°F) for 45-50 minutes or until cooked.
Serves 6.

Photograph below:
Waist-line Luncheon (Recipe page 184)

Cinnamon Sugar Doughnuts

(Photograph this page)
Delicious served with afternoon tea.

½ cup milk
2 teaspoons sugar
15g (½oz) compressed yeast
2 cups flour
1 teaspoon salt
30g (1oz) butter or margarine
oil for frying
1 teaspoon cinnamon
3 tablespoons sugar

Heat milk to lukewarm add sugar and yeast and stir well until sugar has dissolved. Stand in a warm position until bubbles form on the surface, approximately 10 minutes. Combine the flour and salt in a bowl and rub in the butter, add the yeast mixture and work into a manageable dough adding a little extra milk if necessary. Knead on a lightly floured board, until dough forms a ball. Place in a lightly oiled bowl, rubbing the dough with a little oil. Cover, and sit in a warm place until doubled in size, approximately 30 minutes. Re-knead, cut into rounds, deep fry until golden brown and cooked, drain and toss in the combined cinnamon and sugar.
Makes approximately 10.

Fruit and Nut Bun

(Photograph this page)
A delicious bun for afternoon tea.

3 cups self-raising flour
½ teaspoon salt
1 teaspoon mixed spice
60g (2oz) butter or margarine
⅓ cup sugar
1 egg
¾ cup milk
¾ cup sultanas

Icing:

1 cup icing sugar, sifted
1 tablespoon warm water
red food colouring
glacé cherries
walnuts

Combine the flour, salt and spice in a bowl and rub in the butter until the mixture resembles fine breadcrumbs. Add the sugar, egg, milk and sultanas and knead into a soft manageable dough. Shape into a 15cm (6") round and mark with an X on the top. Place on a greased baking sheet, brush with milk and bake at 180°C (350°F) for 50 minutes or until cooked. Make the icing by combining the sugar and water and adding sufficient food colouring to obtain a pale pink colour. Drizzle over the bun and decorate with glacé cherries and walnuts.

Honey and Sultana Scones

(Photograph this page)
This recipe is ideal made in a food processor.

½ cup natural yoghurt
1 tablespoon honey
½ cup milk
3 cups self-raising flour
½ teaspoon salt
¾ cup sultanas

Combine the yoghurt and honey in a bowl, then beat in the milk, flour and salt. Stir in the sultanas and knead dough on a lightly-floured board and shape into a round approximately 1½cm (1") thick. Cut into rounds and place on a lightly greased baking sheet. Glaze with a little milk and bake at 200°C (400°F) for 10 minutes or until golden brown and cooked.
Makes approximately 16.

Parsley Scones

(Photograph this page)
2 cups self-raising flour
seasoning to taste
2 tablespoons finely chopped parsley
½ onion, finely chopped
3 shallots, chopped
30g (1oz) butter or margarine
150ml (¼ pint) milk
extra milk for glazing

Combine the flour, seasoning, parsley, onion and shallots in a bowl, rub in the butter until the mixture resembles fine breadcrumbs then add sufficient milk to make a soft but manageable dough. Knead on a lightly-floured board, approximately 2½cm (1") thick. Cut into rounds and place on a greased baking sheet, glaze with a little milk and bake at 200°C (400°F) for 12-15 minutes or until cooked.
Make approximately 12.

Photograph page 188:
Post Office, Anakie Gemfields, Sapphire, Queensland.

Photograph page 189:
Barley fields, Petersville, South Australia.

Photograph this page:
Left: Fruit and Nut Bun
Second left: Parsley Scones
Third left: Cinnamon Sugar Doughnuts
Front: Honey and Sultana Scones

Spiced Carrot Cake

The combination of carrot and raisins add a luscious flavour to this spiced cake.

125g (4oz) butter or margarine
½ cup honey
1 teaspoon vanilla essence
2 eggs, beaten
1½ cups grated carrot
½ cup chopped raisins
½ cup walnuts
1¼ cups wholemeal flour
2½ teaspoons baking powder
½ teaspoon bicarbonate soda
1 teaspoon cinnamon
½ teaspoon allspice
¼ cup milk
2 teaspoons lemon juice

Cream butter, honey and vanilla together until light and fluffy then beat in eggs. Add carrot, raisins and walnuts and beat well. Add sifted dry ingredients alternately with milk and lemon juice. Spoon into a greased and lined 20cm (8") x 10cm (4") loaf tin. Bake at 160°C (325°F) for approximately 1¼-1½ hours. Cool in tin before turning out.
Makes 1 carrot cake.

Wholemeal Cheese Scones

Delicious spread with butter or peanut butter for afternoon tea.

1½ cups self-raising flour
½ cup wholemeal self-raising flour
¼ teaspoon salt
30g (1oz) butter or margarine
¾-1 cup milk
½ cup grated cheese
sesame seeds

Sift flours and salt together and rub in the butter. Heat the milk and add to the dry ingredients with the cheese and mix to a soft manageable dough. Turn onto a floured board and knead until smooth. Roll out 2cm (¾") thick and cut into shapes using a 6cm (2½") cutter. Place on a baking sheet, brush tops with milk and sprinkle with sesame seeds. Bake at 220°C (440°F) for 12-15 minutes or until golden.
Makes 12.

Photograph opposite page:
"Jim Jim Falls," Kakadu National Park, Northern Territory.

Photograph this page:
"Trephina Gorge," near Alice Springs, Northern Territory.

Malt Bread

This is an old favourite, and always popular for afternoon tea.

1 teaspoon bicarbonate of soda
pinch salt
2 cups self-raising flour
1 cup bran
1 tablespoon butter or margarine
1 tablespoon golden syrup
1 teaspoon malt
1¼ cups milk

Add soda and salt to the flour and mix well with the bran. Rub in the butter. Melt the golden syrup and malt over a low heat and mix well into dry ingredients. Lastly add the milk. Pour into a well greased large nut loaf tin with lid on, or two small tins, and bake at 180°C (350°F) for approximately 45-60 minutes. Cool in the tin, and serve when cold, sliced and buttered.
Make 1 loaf.

Shortbread

250g (8oz) butter, cubed
⅓ cup caster sugar
½ teaspoon vanilla essence
2¼ cups flour
1 tablespoon cornflour

For Decoration:

glacé cherries or almonds

Cream butter, sugar and vanilla together until light and fluffy. Add flours, mix until ingredients are well combined. Press mixture into a 20cm (8") square cake tin and cut into small fingers. Prick each piece with a fork to form a pattern and decorate with a glacé cherry or almond. Sprinkle with caster sugar and bake at 150°C (300°F) for 30-40 minutes or until cooked. Makes 1 x 20cm (8") square shortbread.

Wheatgerm Walnut Slice

2 large apples, peeled, finely chopped
⅓ cup water
½ cup brown sugar
1 cup raisins
1 tablespoon cornflour
1½ cups flour
1 teaspoon baking powder
½ teaspoon bicarbonate of soda
pinch salt
1 cup brown sugar
1 cup finely chopped walnuts
1 cup wheatgerm
185g (6oz) butter or margarine

Place apples, water and brown sugar in a saucepan and simmer until the apples are tender, then add the raisins. Blend cornflour with some liquid from the apples, add to the pan and stir until thickened, allow to cool. Sift flour, baking powder, bicarbonate of soda and salt into a bowl, add brown sugar, walnuts and wheatgerm and rub in the butter. Press ⅔ of the mixture into the base of a 27cm (11″) x 18cm (7″) lamington tin. Place apple mixture over base and sprinkle over remaining crumb mixture. Bake at 190°C (375°F) for 40-50 minutes or until cooked. Serve cold.
Makes 1 slice.

Spicy Fruit Crisps

1 cup self-raising flour
¾ cup coconut
¾ cup sugar
2 teaspoons mixed spice
60g (2oz) butter or margarine
1 tablespoon golden syrup
¼ teaspoon bicarbonate of soda
1 egg
1 cup cornflakes
½ cup currants

Combine flour, coconut, sugar and mixed spice in a bowl. Melt the butter and golden syrup over a low heat then stir in the soda; allow to cool. Add egg and melted butter mixture to dry ingredients together with the cornflakes and currants. Place teaspoons of mixture onto lightly greased baking sheets, allowing room for spreading. Bake at 180°C (350°F) for 15-20 minutes or until golden brown, leave on trays 5 minutes before removing.
Makes approximately 40.

Photograph below:
Opal Mines, Coober Pedy, South Australia.

Muesli Squares

A tasty addition to any lunchbox.
90g (3oz) butter or margarine
¼ cup brown sugar
1 egg, beaten
1 cup flour
pinch salt
1 teaspoon baking powder
1 cup muesli

Cream the butter and sugar together until light and fluffy. Add the egg and beat well. Sift flour, salt and baking powder together and gently stir into creamed mixture, adding the muesli. Roll out onto floured board and cut into squares or fingers. If the mixture is too sticky, refrigerate before rolling. Place squares on a baking sheet and bake at 160°C (325°F) for 15-20 minutes. Cool on rack and store in an airtight container.
Makes approximately 24.

Photograph opposite:
Wheat Harvesting, Mooree, New South Wales.

Photograph page 196/197:
Lorne Hill Gorge, near Cooktown, Northern Queensland.

Anzac Biscuits

2 cups rolled oats
½ cup sugar
1 cup flour
125g (4oz) butter, melted
1 tablespoon golden syrup
1 teaspoon bicarbonate of soda
2 tablespoons boiling water

Combine the oats, sugar, flour and melted butter together. Then add golden syrup and lastly the soda dissolved in the boiling water. Place spoonfuls of mixture onto a greased sheet and bake at 180°C (350°F) for 15-20 minutes or until cooked.
Makes approximately 12-18.

Walnut Bread

1 egg
¾ cup brown sugar
½ cup milk
1 cup flour
1 cup self-raising flour
pinch salt
½ cup chopped walnuts

Beat egg and sugar together then add the milk. Gradually blend in the sifted flours and salt then the walnuts. Place in a well greased loaf tin and bake at 180°C (350°F) for 30-40 minutes. Serve when cold, sliced and buttered.
Makes 1 loaf.

Wholemeal Fruit Slice

This slice is delicious served with tea or coffee.

1 cup raw sugar
1 cup wholemeal flour
1 cup desiccated coconut
1 cup mixed fruit
1 cup milk
12 dried apricots, finely chopped

Mix all the ingredients together and place in a greased lamington tin. Bake at 150°C (300°F) for 40-45 minutes or until cooked. Cut into fingers before the slice cools.
Makes 1 slice.

Avocado and Walnut Spread

(Photograph page 204/205)
Use this in place of butter on bread particularly good for asparagus rolls.

1 ripe avocado, peeled, mashed
1-2 tablespoons lemon juice
salt to taste
2 tablespoons finely chopped walnuts
1 shallot, finely chopped

Combine avocado with the lemon juice and salt, cover and chill. Stir in the walnuts and shallot. Adjust seasoning and serve with cracker biscuits.

Date and Peanut Butter Spread

(Photograph page 204/205)
Particularly tasty on fresh wholemeal bread.

1 cup pitted dates, roughly chopped
¾ cup water
salt to taste
smooth peanut butter

Place dates and water in a saucepan. Bring to the boil and cook 5-8 minutes, stirring frequently. Add a little salt to taste. Allow to cool, then stir in sufficient peanut butter to make a spreading consistency for sandwiches, rolls, etc.

Chick Pea and Tahini Paste

(Photograph page 204/205)
155g (5oz) chick peas
juice 2 lemons
2 cloves garlic, crushed
90g (3oz) sesame tahini paste
salt to taste
olive oil
paprika
finely chopped parsley
wholemeal pita bread

Soak peas for about 12 hours, then cook until tender. Use a pressure cooker if desired. Strain and reserve liquid. Puree 4 tablespoons of chick pea liquid with the lemon juice, garlic and chick peas in a blender or food processor. Add the tahini paste and blend until smooth, then add the remainder with a little extra liquid if the mixture is too thick. Season and spoon into small bowls and cover with thin layer of oil. Garnish with paprika and chopped parsley and serve as a dip with pita bread.

Photograph below:
Rice field, New South Wales.

Peanut Butter and Pineapple Spread

(Photograph page 204/205)
This spread is best used immediately.

¼ cup crunchy peanut butter
½ cup unsweetened crushed pineapple, drained

Combine the peanut butter with the pineapple and use as a spread on toast, rye breads, wholemeal muffins or in sandwiches with lettuce or chopped parsley.

Photograph opposite:
The view from "Devil's Coach House" looking to The Blue Lake, Jenolan Caves, New South Wales.

Photograph pages 200/201:
Sunset on Lake Monger, Perth, Western Australia.

Photograph pages 202/203:
Sorghum Field, Darling Downs, Queensland.

COOKING NATURALLY

This section of the book is devoted to the wonderful, often neglected area of Vegetable and Dairy Cookery.

Vegetables in particular have the most varied and abundant source of nourishment and are prized as highly as meats in some parts of the world. In Australia there are still market gardens and cattle grazing on the outskirts of our cities and there are little roadside stalls with freshly laid eggs and fruit and vegetables "just picked" from the garden.

With the migration of new settlers from Europe and Asia, many different varieties of vegetables have sprung up in our shops and market gardens. Therefore vegetables have been introduced in numerous ways to every variety of dish instead of just as an accompaniment to meat. Baby squash, zucchini, tiny tomatoes and cucumbers are becoming more and more common in our daily diet.

Dairy foods need little introduction as they are so versatile and may be disguised to suit any occasion — fondues, cheese platters and dips for the patio lunch or unexpected guests. Turn the pages and become inspired by the recipes from the great wealth of our Australian pastures and small farming communities.

Photograph opposite:
Nature at its best.
Fresh foods a'plenty

Minted Pea Chowder

A quick and easy soup, making good use of nutritious fresh vegetables.

2 onions
1 carrot
2 sticks celery, trimmed
2 potatoes
3 tablespoons butter or margarine
6 cups water
seasoning to taste
2 cups frozen peas
2 tablespoons flour
1 tablespoon chopped mint
½ cup cream

Chop all fresh vegetables roughly. Melt butter in a large saucepan. Add chopped vegetables and sauté for 5 minutes. Add water, seasoning and bring to the boil. Simmer gently for 20 minutes. Add peas and continue simmering for 10 minutes. Strain the vegetables and puree in a food processor or through a coarse sieve. Gradually blend flour with a little of the hot vegetable stock to form a smooth paste and stir into the vegetables with the remaining stock. Return to the saucepan with the mint and bring to the boil. Cook for two minutes. Swirl in the cream and serve garnished with sprigs of mint. Serves 8.

Pumpkin Vichysoisse

(Photograph this page)
500g (1lb) peeled, seeded pumpkin
250g (8oz) chopped washed leeks
8 cups chicken stock
1 teaspoon salt
cayenne pepper to taste
½ cup cream or yoghurt
½ teaspoon paprika

Place all ingredients except the seasoning into suitably sized saucepan. Bring to the boil and cook until the pumpkin is tender. Remove from the heat, add seasonings, blend until smooth, then add the cream. Serve garnished with chopped parsley or chopped chives. Serves 6.

Leek and Tomato Soup

Leeks make a nice change from onions and are a good combination with tomatoes.

3 leeks, washed finely, chopped
5 cups chicken stock
1kg (2lb) tomatoes
1 teaspoon salt
½ teaspoon lemon pepper
1 teaspoon chopped basil

Place the finely chopped leeks in a saucepan and cover with the chicken stock. Bring to the boil. Cook for a further five minutes, then add tomatoes. Simmer until the tomatoes are tender. Remove from the heat, add seasonings and serve. Serves 6.

Tomato Refresher

This is a quick and easy "no cook" soup that could also be served as a drink with the addition of a splash of vodka.

1 large orange, peeled, chopped
1 red apple, peeled, cored, diced
500g (1lb) ripe tomatoes, peeled chopped
1 small onion, diced
2 cloves garlic, crushed
½ teaspoon salt
1 cup chicken stock
1 tablespoon lemon juice

Blend all the ingredients together in a food processor until smooth. Pour into a large bowl and chill until required. Serves 4.

Photograph below:
Pumpkin Vichysoisse (Recipe this page)

Minestrone Soup

(Photograph page 212/213)

A hearty, filling soup, good for lunch on the run.

2 tablespoons butter or margarine
4 carrots, sliced
4 sticks celery, sliced
2 potatoes, roughly chopped
3 onions, roughly chopped
2 cloves garlic, crushed
3 rashers bacon, roughly chopped
14 cups beef stock
1 x 220g (7oz) can* red kidney beans
1 x 440g (14oz) can* peeled tomatoes
¾ cup macaroni
¼ cup chopped parsley
seasoning to taste

Nearest equivalent can size.

Melt the butter in a saucepan and sauté the vegetables and bacon until tender. Add the stock, beans and tomatoes. Bring to the boil, cover and simmer for 30 minutes. Add macaroni and simmer uncovered, until tender. Serve in deep bowls, sprinkled with parsley.
Serves 10-12.

Cream of Carrot and Honey Soup

(Photograph page 212/213)
500g (1lb) baby carrots
4 cups vegetable stock
¼ cup honey
3 cloves garlic, crushed
salt
mace
150ml (¼ pint) cream
chopped parsley

Slice carrots into a saucepan with the vegetable stock, honey, garlic and salt. Bring to the boil, reduce heat and simmer 30 minutes or until carrots are tender. Adjust seasonings to taste. Puree in a blender or food processor and gently reheat before stirring in the cream. Do not boil. Serve sprinkled with chopped parsley.
Serves 6.

Photograph below:
Sultana grapes,
Mildura, Victoria.

Brussel Sprouts Soup

(Photograph page 212/213)
2 tablespoons butter or oil
1 onion, finely sliced
1kg (2lb) brussels sprouts
4 cups chicken stock
¼ cup cream

Melt the butter in a saucepan and saute onion until tender. Add brussels sprouts and stock and bring to the boil. Reduce the heat and simmer for 10-20 minutes or until cooked. Puree in a food processor or through a sieve. Reheat and serve with a swirl of cream.
Serves 4.

Photograph page 208:
Bendigo Pottery, Victoria.

Photograph page 211:
The peaceful waters of
The Midlands, Tasmania.

Photograph page 212/213:
(Recipe this page)
Left: Brussels Sprouts Soup
Centre: Minestrone Soup
Right: Cream of Carrot and Honey Soup

Stir-Fried Vegetables

(Photograph page 222 / 223)
Serve this colourful dish as a main course or with Chinese noodles. Delicious!

3 tablespoons vegetable oil
1 nob root ginger, peeled, finely sliced
1 clove garlic, crushed
2 sticks celery, diagonally sliced
½ red capsicum, seeded, sliced
1 cup peas
1 zucchini, thinly sliced
6 brussel sprouts, quartered
1 carrot finely sliced
1 cup button mushrooms, sliced
1 leek, finely sliced
1 cup bean shoots
1 cup raw cashews
½ cup water
3 teaspoons soy sauce
2 teaspoons cornflour

Heat the oil in a frying pan or wok, add the ginger and garlic and cook for 30 seconds. Stir in the remaining vegetables and nuts and simmer until tender. Combine the water, soy sauce and cornflour and add to the vegetables. Allow to simmer for a few minutes, then serve.
Serves 2-4.

Crunchy Vegetables

(Photograph page 222 / 223)
The macadamia nuts add a lovely texture and crunch to these vegetables.

2 tablespoons vegetable oil
1 onion, finely sliced
1 carrot, sliced
1 parsnip, peeled, sliced
1 zucchini, sliced
1 teaspoon dill
½ cup macadamia nuts

Heat oil in a frying pan or wok and saute the onion, carrot and parsnip for 2-3 minutes. Add zucchini, dill and macadamia nuts and continue cooking for a further 3-4 minutes. Do not overcook. Serve immediately.
Serves 3-4.

Spiced Zucchini Crepes

The Filling:

1 tablespoon butter
1 leek, washed, chopped
500g (1lb) zucchini, sliced
½ teaspoon ground allspice
1 egg, lightly beaten
8 x 18cm (7") crepes
seasoning to taste

Melt butter in a saucepan. Add leek and zucchini and saute until tender. Puree in a food processor or through a sieve. Season and beat in the egg. Divide the filling between the crepes, fold and place in a dish.
Reheat at 180°C (350°F) for 20 minutes covered with foil, or in the microwave for 2-3 minutes.
Serves 8.

Sweet Potato with Sesame Seeds

(Photograph page 222 / 223)
A unique and tasty way to serve this vegetable.

3 tablespoons vegetable oil
1 large sweet potato, peeled, thinly sliced
1 leek, washed, sliced
2 teaspoons sesame seeds
seasoning to taste
1 cup snow peas
1 teaspoon dill

Heat the oil in a frying pan or wok and saute the potato and leek until tender. Add sesame seeds, seasoning, snow peas and dill. Cook for 1 minute, then serve immediately. Do not overcook the snow peas.
Serves 3-4.

Chicken Pie

(Photograph page 217)
1 tablespoon butter or margarine
1 onion, finely sliced
2 rashers bacon, sliced
1 cup mushrooms, finely sliced
¼ cup finely chopped parsley
2 tablespoons butter or margarine
2 tablespoons flour
1 cup chicken stock
1 tablespoon white wine
seasoning to taste
500g (1lb) cooked diced chicken
1 sheet ready rolled puff pastry
beaten egg for glazing

Melt 1 tablespoon butter and saute onion until soft. Add the bacon, mushrooms and parsley. In another pan make the sauce by melting 2 tablespoons butter, adding flour and making a roux. Add chicken stock stirring continuously and cooking until thick and boiling. Reduce heat, add wine and season to taste. Mix together bacon, mushroom mixture and chicken. Add to sauce and spoon into pie dish. Cover with pastry, decorate and glaze with beaten egg. Bake at 200°C (400°F) for 5 minutes, reduce temperature to 180°C (350°F) for remaining 20 minutes. Serve hot with vegetables or your favourite salad.
Serves 4.

Chicken Cabbage Rolls

This mixture can also be used with vine leaves as a filling for dolmades, to be served with drinks.

1kg (2lb) chicken mince
3 shallots, chopped
1 teaspoon salt
1 teaspoon green peppercorns
1 teaspoon wheatgerm
1 teaspoon chicken stock
6 large cabbage leaves, blanched

Combine the chicken with shallots, salt and green peppercorns. Add wheatgerm to make a firm mixture. Open out the cabbage leaves and divide chicken mixture evenly over each one. Roll up and secure and place in a baking dish. Brush with the chicken stock and bake at 180°C (350°F) for approx. 20 minutes or until cooked.
Serves 6.

Photograph page 214:
Homemade Ice Cream and
Selected Fruits.

Photograph page 215:
Aboriginal "Elder",
Darwin, Northern Territory.

Photograph below:
Red Sands of the Simpson
Desert, South Australia.

Chicken and Parsley Dumplings

(Photograph page 217)
1½kg (3lb) chicken jointed,
skin removed
1 cup white wine
water or stock to cover chicken
1 small onion, sliced
3 sprigs parsley
2 sticks celery, sliced
1 bay leaf
5 peppercorns
2 teaspoons salt
seasoning to taste
paprika

Dumplings:

2 cups self-raising flour
1 tablespoon butter or margarine
½ teaspoon salt
1 tablespoon chopped parsley
1 cup milk
3 tablespoons cornflour
seasoning to taste
paprika
parsley sprigs for garnish

Place chicken in a shallow baking dish add wine, water, onion, parsley, celery, bay leaf, peppercorns and salt. Cover and bake at 120°C (250°F) for 1½- 2 hours or until chicken is cooked. Skim off fat. While chicken is cooking prepare the dumplings. Sift the flour and rub in the butter. Add the salt and parsley and milk. Drop the dumplings in on top of the chicken. (They should not sink in.) Cook for 20 minutes or until dumplings have risen and browned. Remove chicken and dumplings and keep warm. Strain liquid and blend cornflour with a little water or wine and add to the liquid. Combine and season. Bring to the boil and pour gravy over chicken and dumplings. Dust with paprika and garnish with parsley.
Serves 4.

Photograph opposite:
Top: Chicken and Parsley Dumplings
(Recipe this page)
Bottom: Chicken Pie
(Recipe this page)

Photograph page 218/219:
Port Stephens, New South Wales.

Tomato and Cheese Quiche

(Photograph this page)

The Pastry:

3 tablespoons butter or margarine
1 cup flour
¼ teaspoon salt
2 tablespoons iced water

The Fillings:

4 rashers bacon, chopped
4 shallots, chopped
4 eggs
1 tablespoon cornflour
¼ teaspoon lemon thyme
1½ cups cream
½ cup milk
⅔ cup grated tasty cheese
seasoning to taste
1 large tomato, sliced
1 tablespoon chopped parsley

Make the pastry by rubbing the butter into the flour and salt then add water and mix to a firm dough. Knead lightly and chill for 30 minutes. Line a 20cm (8″) quiche tin with the pastry and bake blind at 200°C (400°F) for 8 minutes. Cool. Saute bacon and half the shallots, until bacon is cooked. Beat together the eggs, cornflour and lemon thyme and add cream, milk and seasoning. Pour into prepared quiche tin and sprinkle with cheese. Arrange tomato slices over mixture, sprinkle with remaining shallots and parsley. Bake at 180°C (350°F) for 20-25 minutes or until set. Serve either hot or cold.
Serves 4-6.

Egg and Bacon Pie

(Photograph this page)

The Pastry:

185g (6oz) self-raising flour
60g (2oz) flour
½ level teaspoon salt
125g (4oz) butter or margarine
5 tablespoons cold water

The Filling:

4 eggs
seasoning to taste
6 tablespoons milk
185g (6oz) bacon, chopped
beaten egg for glazing

Sift together flours and salt and rub butter into flour mixture. Make a well in the centre, add water and stir into the flour, mix to firm dough. Turn out onto a floured board, shape into a ball and halve. Roll each piece to ½cm (¼″) thickness to fit a 20cm (8″) pie plate. Line the plate with one half of the pastry, and whisk the eggs and seasoning and milk. Arrange the bacon in the bottom of the pastry case and pour over the egg mixture. Cut remaining pastry into strips and lattice the top of the pie. Glaze with beaten egg and bake at 200°C (400°F) for 15 minutes. Reduce to 175°C (340°F) and cook for a further 15-20 minutes or until set.
Serves 4-6.

Photograph below:
(Recipes this page)
Top left: Tomato and Cheese Quiche.
Top right: Eggs on Cocotte.
Bottom: Egg and Bacon Pie.

Eggs on Cocotte

(Photograph this page)

2 tablespoons butter or margarine
6 shallots, chopped
125g (4oz) mushrooms, sliced
½ cup chopped ham or salami
4 eggs
seasoning to taste
4 tablespoons cream or yoghurt
grated Parmesan cheese

Melt butter in pan and saute shallots until soft. Add mushrooms and ham and cook a further 2 minutes. Spoon mixture evenly between four individual ramekins and break an egg into each one. Season. Spoon 1 tablespoon of cream or yoghurt over each egg and sprinkle with grated Parmesan cheese. Cook at 180°C (350°F) for 12-15 minutes or until eggs are set. Serve accompanied with hot buttered toast.
Serves 4.

Photograph opposite:
Bunyeroo Valley, Wilpena Pound,
Flinders Ranges, South Australia.

Photograph page 222/223
(Recipes page 214)
Top left: Stir-Fried Vegetables
Right: Crunchy Vegetables
Front: Sweet Potato with Sesame Seeds

Chicken Puff Kiev

90g (3oz) unsalted butter or margarine
1 clove garlic, crushed
2 shallots, chopped
1 tablespoon parsley, chopped
2 teaspoons Worcestershire sauce
¼ teaspoon black pepper
4 whole breasts of chicken, skinned, boned
2 sheets ready rolled puff pastry
milk or cream for glazing.

Cream the butter, garlic, shallots, parsley, Worcestershire sauce and pepper together and shape into a 28cm (11") oblong. Wrap in foil and freeze until firm. Pound out chicken breasts until very thin with a meat mallet or rolling pin. Cut frozen butter mixture into 4 equal portions. Place one portion in the centre of each chicken breast and fold chicken over butter so that it is completely encased and makes a roll shape. Cut pastry sheets in half and place a chicken roll on each strip of pastry. Roll up firmly. Place seam-side down on a baking sheet. Glaze with milk or cream and bake at 230°C (450°F) for 20-25 minutes or until pastry is golden brown.
Serves 4.

Macaroni Slaw Salad

1⅓ cups cooked macaroni
1 cup grated cabbage
¼ cup grated carrot
¼ grated capsicum
90g (3oz) ham, chopped
2 hard boiled eggs, sliced
1 tablespoon mayonnaise
1 tablespoon cider vinegar
1 tablespoon tomato sauce
¼ teaspoon tarragon
2 lettuce cups
sprigs of herbs to garnish

Combine the macaroni with the cabbage, carrot, capsicum, ham and eggs. Combine the mayonnaise with the vinegar, tomato sauce and tarragon. Pour over the macaroni and toss together thoroughly. Serve, spooned into the lettuce cups and garnish with sprigs of herbs.
Serves 2.

Mozzarella Melters

125g (4oz) butter or margarine softened
seasoning to taste
1-2 cloves garlic, crushed
8 slices bread
8 slices salami
2 tomatoes, sliced
1 onion, finely sliced
8 olives, stoned, chopped
250g (½1b) Mozzarella cheese, thinly sliced

Cream butter, seasoning and garlic together till creamy. Spread evenly over both sides of bread, taking care to spread to the edges. Place bread on a baking sheet and top each piece with slices of salami, tomatoes, onion and olives. Top with the cheese and bake at 190°C (375°F) for 20 minutes. Serve cut in half diagonally.
Serves 8.

Photograph below:
A relaxing picnic in the country.

Mustard Beefsteak Pie

3 tablespoons butter or margarine
2 tablespoons prepared mustard
250g (8oz) blade steak cubed
4 rashers bacon, chopped
1 onion, sliced
2 tablespoons flour
½ cup liquid reserved
125g (4oz) can* golden butter
beans, drained,
125g (4oz) matured Cheddar cheese
cubed
1 x 375g (12oz) packet frozen puff
pastry, thawed
1 egg yolk
1 tablespoon milk

*Nearest equivalent can size.

Melt the butter with the mustard in a
heavy based frying pan. Add meat,
bacon and onion and sauté for 3-4
minutes. Stir in flour and cook for 2
minutes. Add reserved bean liquid,
stir constantly and bring to the boil.
Add mushrooms and beans and
simmer for a further 5 minutes. Add
the cheese. Roll half the pastry out
and use to line a 20cm (8") pie dish.
Spoon in filling, moisten edges with a
little water. Roll out remaining pastry
and use to cover the pie. Trim edges,
seal well and decorate. Refrigerate
for 15 minutes. Combine egg yolk
with milk and glaze the pie. Bake at
200°C (400°F) for 25-30 minutes or
until pastry is golden brown.
Serves 6.

Bacon and Egg Baskets

6 soft hamburger buns
3 tablespoons butter or margarine
2 teaspoons Worcestershire sauce
6 eggs
3 rashers bacon, chopped
1 onion, sliced
seasoning to taste
250g (8oz) processed Cheddar
cheese, grated

Cut a slice from the top of each bun
and reserve. Hollow out each bun,
leaving a thick shell. Melt the butter
in a saucepan and stir in the
Worcestershire sauce. Brush inside of
buns with butter mixture and
carefully break an egg into each one.
Sauté bacon and onion in frying pan,
drain well and spoon over the eggs.
Season, top with cheese and replace
lids. Brush with remaining butter.
Bake at 200°C (400°F) for 15 minutes
or until the egg has cooked. Serve
hot or cold.
Serves 6.

Savoury Tomato Quiche

1 cup flour
pinch salt
60g (2oz) butter or margarine, cubed
2-3 tablespoons water
3 tablespoons Parmesan cheese
1 tablespoon parsley, chopped
2 tablespoons oil
1 large onion, finely chopped
2 cloves garlic
4 tomatoes, chopped
1 tablespoon tomato paste
1 teaspoon basil
1 teaspoon sugar
2 eggs
seasoning to taste

Make a pastry in the usual way,
with the flour, salt, butter, water,
1 tablespoon of Parmesan cheese and
the parsley. Knead lightly together
until smooth, roll out onto a floured
board and use to line a 20cm (8")
quiche tin. Prick pastry well, with a
fork and refrigerate for 10 minutes.
Bake at 180°C (350°F) for 15 minutes or
until pastry is pale, golden brown.
Heat oil in frying pan and sauté the
onion and garlic until tender.
Remove pan from heat and stir in the
tomatoes and remaining ingredients.
Pour into (prepared) case and bake
at 180°C (350°F) for approximately 40
minutes or until cooked.
Serves 4-6.

Cheesy Zucchini Lamb

1.5kg (3lb) leg lamb, boned, cubed
2 tablespoons seasoned flour
4 tablespoons butter or margarine
2 onions, chopped
60g (2oz) Hungarian salami, chopped
2 cloves garlic, crushed
1½cups beef stock
seasoning to taste
½ cup rice
3 zucchini, sliced
125g (4oz) Cheddar cheese, grated
2 tablespoons grated Parmesan
cheese

Toss meat in flour and brown in 3
tablespoons of the butter. Add
onion, salami and garlic and sauté 2
minutes. Stir in stock and bring to
simmering point. Spoon into a large
casserole. Cover and bake at 180°C
(350°F) for 30 minutes. Season and stir
in rice. Cook for a further 15 minutes.
Sauté the zucchini in remaining
butter, stir the casserole and arrange
the zucchini on top. Sprinkle with the
cheeses and bake a further 5-10
minutes.
Serves 4-6.

Photograph below:
Tossed Green Salad
with Yoghurt Dressing.

Simple Cheddar Soufflé

3 tablespoons butter or margarine
¼ cup flour
1 cup milk
125g (4oz) Cheddar cheese, grated
¼ teaspoon dry mustard
pinch cayenne pepper
1½ teaspoons salt
3 eggs, separated

Melt the butter in a saucepan and blend in flour. Cook 1-2 minutes, then whisk in the milk. Stir constantly over moderate heat until smooth and boiling. Briskly beat in cheese and seasonings. Cool, then beat in egg yolks. Whisk egg whites until stiff, then fold into the sauce. Pour into a medium sized, greased soufflé dish. Bake at 160°C (325°F) for 50-60 minutes. Serve immediately with a tossed salad and hot, crusty bread.
Serves 4.

Baked Zucchini with Mushrooms

(Photograph this page)

60g (2oz) butter or margarine
250g (8oz) mushrooms, sliced
½ teaspoon salt
1 clove garlic, crushed
pepper
¼ teaspoon oregano
3 large zucchini, coarsely grated
¼ cup soft breadcrumbs
4 tablespoons Parmesan cheese, grated
1 tablespoon cream
4 eggs, beaten

Melt butter in a large saucepan add mushrooms and cook until most of the liquid has evaporated. Add salt, garlic, pepper and oregano.

Combine zucchini, breadcrumbs, 2 tablespoons Parmesan cheese and mushroom mixture and spoon into an ovenproof dish. Pour combined cream and eggs over zucchini mixture and bake at 180°C (350°F) for 25-30 minutes. Cut into squares and top with remaining cheese. Serve with a salad of your choice.
Serves 6-8.

Photograph below:
Top: Buttered Leeks.
Bottom: Baked Zucchini with Mushrooms.

Buttered Leeks

(Photograph this page)
1 tablespoon finely chopped onion
1 clove garlic, crushed
3 tablespoons butter or margarine
6 leeks, washed trimmed cut in half lengthwise
seasoning to taste

Lightly saute onion and garlic in a little of the butter until softened. Place leeks into boiling salted water and reduce heat to simmer and cook 2-3 minutes. Drain and refresh in cold water. Place in a greased shallow casserole dish, dot with butter and sprinkle with seasoning. Cover with a lid or foil and cook at 180°C (350°F) for 20 minutes. Serve hot as a side dish for roast meats.

Roast Veal Rouladen

1.5kg (3lb) leg veal boned
4 rashers bacon
¼ cup brandy

The Sauce:

½ cup chopped shallots
250g (8oz) mushrooms, thinly sliced
2 tablespoons flour
1 teaspoon dried basil
1¼ cups cream

Form veal neatly into a roll. Wrap bacon rashers around it, securing with wooden toothpicks. Place in a greased baking dish. Pour in brandy and cover with foil. Bake at 180°C (350°F) for 1½ hours. Remove foil and bake for a further hour or until veal is sufficiently cooked. Keep warm on a serving dish while preparing sauce.

Reduce pan juices by half. Add shallots and mushrooms and saute for 2-3 minutes. Blend in flour and basil and cook 1 minute. Remove from heat and stir in the cream. Return to a low heat and stir constantly until sauce thickens. Carve the meat and serve accompanied with the sauce. Serves 6.

Photograph page 232/233:
Perth by night.

Photograph page 234/235:
Australian National Library
from Commonwealth Gardens Canberra.

Choc-Rum Delights

These are delicious served with coffee.

1 x 400g (13oz) can* condensed milk
1 x 100g (3oz) block dark chocolate
1 tablespoon gelatine
2 tablespoons water
2 tablespoons rum

*Nearest equivalent can size.

Combine condensed milk and chocolate in a saucepan and heat gently until chocolate melts. Dissolve gelatine in hot water and stir into the chocolate mixture with the rum. Pour into a wetted 18cm (7") square cake tin and refrigerate overnight. Cut into squares and serve decorated as desired, by tossing in toasted ground almonds, sieved icing sugar or chopped unblanched almonds.
Makes 36.

Caramel Peaches "n" Cherries

3 tablespoons butter or margarine
½ cup brown sugar
1 x 425g (13oz) can* cherries, drained
½ cup liquid reserved
1 x 425g (13oz) can* peach halves, drained, ½ cup liquid reserved

*Nearest equivalent can size.

Melt butter in a frying pan and stir in the sugar and cherry liquid. Stir over a medium heat for 5 minutes. Add remaining fruit and liquid and continue cooking for a further 2 minutes until fruit has heated through.
Serves 4-6.

Plaited Plum Strudel

A lovely, light pastry dessert in which fresh plums may be used as an alternative, when in season.

125g (4oz) butter or margarine
2 cups fresh wholemeal breadcrumbs
2 tablespoons brown sugar
1 tablespoon finely grated lemon rind
1 x 825g (24oz) can dark plums, drained, stoned, liquid reserved
6 sheets filo pastry
¼ cup flaked almonds

*Nearest equivalent can size.

Melt half the butter in a medium sized saucepan. Add the breadcrumbs and stir constantly over heat until golden brown. Cool slightly then stir in the sugar and lemon rind. Remove ¼ cup of the crumbs and set aside for topping. Combine the remaining crumbs with the plums. Melt the remaining butter in a separate pan and brush 1 sheet of pastry with butter. Place another sheet directly on top and brush with butter. Spread ⅓ of the plum mixture along the centre and gently shape into a roll. Repeat with the remaining pastry and filling. Place the 3 rolls side by side on a baking sheet and plait together. Tuck ends underneath. Brush the top with any remaining butter and sprinkle with reserved crumbs and flaked almonds. Bake at 200°C (400°F) for 20 minutes and serve dusted with icing sugar, with cream or custard.
Serves 6.

Strawberry Ice

A healthy ice, making good use of natural yoghurt and fresh strawberries.

2 teaspoons gelatine
2 tablespoons boiling water
1 punnet strawberries, hulled
1 carton natural yoghurt
2 egg whites
¼ cup caster sugar

Dissolve gelatine in boiling water and pour into a blender with the strawberries and yoghurt. Blend until smooth. Pour into a shallow dish or ice cream container and freeze until a border of ice crystals form around the edge. Beat mixture with a fork to break up ice crystals. Whisk egg whites until soft peaks form, then gradually add sugar and beat to a firm meringue. Carefully fold into the strawberry mixture and freeze for several hours until just firm. Spoon into chilled serving bowls and serve decorated with fresh strawberries
Serves 6-8.

Photograph page 236/237:
"Ayres Rock", Uluru National Park, Northern Territory.

Photograph opposite:
Burra Lake, South Australia.

AUSTRALIANS ON THE MOVE

Many Australians lead such a hectic lifestyle that anything which is time saving, convenient and with little effort involved, is naturally desirable. Therefore life in the 1980's without a microwave is almost unthinkable.

It is the most exciting culinary innovation we have seen for decades. Its many advantages include speed, convenience, coolness, cleanliness and economy. The changeover from conventional cooking to microwave should not be of any concern, as the cooking time is reduced by a third. Frozen foods may be defrosted easily and reheating cold food can be *done* in minutes without losing flavour and moisture. The temperature of the interior of the microwave oven remains cool although the food is hot and any spills can be easily cleaned with a damp cloth.

Dishes and utensils are easier and quicker to clean because food does not stick to them and the same dish may be used for both cooking and serving.

Microwave cooking is more electrically efficient because it requires about half the energy used in conventional cooking and is therefore more economical. The microwave is safe to use and can produce the simplest of meals to an exotic banquet with the minimum of fuss.

The following section is full of tempting morsels, cooked in the minimum time which will *definitely* liberate the busy Australian.

Photograph opposite:
"Stars and Stripes" leads "Kookaburra" in the final race, 1987 America's Cup, Fremantle, Western Australia.

Hot Fruit Muesli

Why not serve your muesli hot for a change, adding these nutritious ingredients

½ cup rolled oats
1-2 tablespoons raw sugar or honey
⅓ cup toasted slivered almonds
2 tablespoons wheatgerm
cinnamon or nutmeg to taste
1 orange, peeled, chopped
1 banana, peeled, sliced
⅓ cup raisins
½ apple, cored, roughly chopped
3-4 tablespoons yoghurt
cinnamon or nutmeg for garnish

Place the oats, raw sugar, almonds, wheatgerm and cinnamon in a bowl. Microwave on HIGH for 2 minutes and stir. Add the chopped orange with the banana, raisins and apple and microwave on HIGH for a further 30 seconds-1 minute. Spoon into indivdual bowls, placing a tablespoon of yoghurt on top of each serve. Sprinkle with a little cinnamon or nutmeg and serve hot. Serves 3-4.

Poached Eggs with Caviar

(Photograph this page)
Ideal for a special breakfast or Sunday lunch

⅔ cup hot water
½ teaspoon vinegar
2 eggs
seasoning to taste
caviar
chives
buttered toast

Combine water and vinegar and pour into the base of 2 ramekins. Microwave on HIGH for 40 seconds, then break an egg into each one. Pierce the yolks carefully with a pin and season. Cover with plastic wrap and microwave on MEDIUM for 1-2 minutes approximately. As soon as the yolks start to change colour, stop cooking. Stand for 1 minute, then remove eggs with slotted spoon. Garnish with some caviar and chives and serve with fingers of toast. Serves 2.

Sultana Plums

(Photograph this page)
A delicious way to serve plums as a quick and easy accompaniment for cereal.

500g (1lb) plums, washed
¼ cup water
¼ cup sugar
1 cup sultanas

Leave plums whole, but pierce each one with a fine skewer and place in a 5 cup casserole dish. Add water and sprinkle with sugar. Cover and microwave on HIGH for 8 minutes. Stir in the sultanas and allow to cool. Serves 4.

Photograph opposite:
Fruit Salad Basket ·
Rum Glazed Cheesecake
(Recipes page 262)

Photograph below:
(Recipes this page)
Poached Eggs with Caviar
Sultana Plums

Cauliflower Soup

A light, easy to make, tasty soup which may be served as an entree or main course.

1 small cauliflower
3 tablespoons chopped shallots
2 tablespoons water
2½ cups hot chicken stock
1 cup milk
1 teaspoon Worcestershire sauce
2 tablespoons flour
seasoning to taste
½ cup grated tasty cheese
2 tablespoons chopped shallots

Trim stalks and break cauliflower into small florets. Combine cauliflower, shallots and water. Cover and microwave for 5 minutes. Drain off liquid and add to the combined stock, ¾ cup of milk and the Worcestershire sauce. Blend the remaining milk with the flour and stir into the liquid.
Cover, microwave until boiling, approximately 10 minutes. Season and pour over the cauliflower. Top with cheese and reheat 3-4 minutes. Serve garnished with shallots.
Serves 3-4.

Tasty Stuffed Potatoes

A hearty lunch time snack that makes an ideal weekend treat.

4 medium potatoes
3 rashers bacon, chopped
1 onion, finely chopped
3 tablespoons sour cream
¼ cup grated cheese
1 tablespoon grated cheese (Reserved)
seasoning to taste
4 shallots, chopped

Scrub potatoes and pierce the skins in several places. Microwave on HIGH for 10 minutes, then allow to cool. Microwave bacon and onion for 3 minutes. Slice top from potatoes, scoop out centres leaving a 1½ cm (1″) wall and combine with the bacon, onion, sour cream, grated cheese and seasoning. Fill cavities of potatoes with bacon mixture, sprinkle with reserved cheese and shallots and reheat for approximately 2 minutes.
Serves 4.

Herbed Scrambled Eggs

(Photograph this page)

Fresh herbs add that special touch and flavour to that family favourite scrambled eggs.

2 eggs
2 tablespoons milk
¼ cup chopped fresh herbs-parsley, thyme, chives
15g (½oz) butter or margarine
seasoning to taste

Beat the eggs with the milk, seasoning and herbs.
Melt the butter in a small 2 cup dish on HIGH for 30 seconds, then pour in the egg mixture. Microwave on MEDIUM for 1-1½ minutes, stirring frequently. Do not overcook. Allow to stand before serving on hot buttered toast or muffins.
Serves 1.

Savoury Muffins

A savoury snack that is not only ideal for breakfast but also as a midday munchie.

2 muffins, halved
4 slices salami
4 slices cheese
1 firm tomato, finely sliced
butter or margarine
seasoning to taste

Butter the muffins and top with the salami and cheese and tomato and season. Place on a plate and microwave on MEDIUM-HIGH for 1½ minutes.
Serves 2.

Cinnamon Banana Muffins

A breakfast suggestion for those with a sweet tooth.

butter or margarine
2 muffins, halved
creamed honey
2 small bananas, finely sliced
cinnamon

Butter the muffins and spread with creamed honey. Top 2 halves with the banana and sprinkle liberally with cinnamon. Cover with remaining muffin. Place on a plate and microwave on MEDIUM-HIGH for 1½ minutes.
Serves 2.

Omelettes

A good omelette deserves a good pan. Keep your omelette pan for omelettes only, and never wash it. Just wipe clean with a damp cloth or paper towel and some salt. There are many types of omelettes and a great variety of fillings.

Basic Omelette:

4 eggs
1½ tablespoons cold water
seasoning to taste
1 tablespoon butter or margarine
seasoning to taste

Break eggs into a basin and beat well with a fork. Add the water and seasoning. Melt butter in an omelette pan. When frothing, pour in egg mixture and leave for about 10-15 seconds, then stir. Lift up the edge of the omelette to let any raw egg run to the edge of the pan. Add the filling; tilt the pan away from you and fold over the omelette to far side, then gently slide on to a hot serving plate.
Serves 2.

Suggested Fillings:

2 tablespoons grated cheese.
Sliced mushrooms saute in butter.
Finely chopped cold chicken.
Chopped bacon.
Chopped prawns.
Chopped ham.

Herbs: Before pouring egg mixture into pan, add a heaped tablespoon of finely chopped chives, parsley, thyme, marjoram etc.
Fish: Use any cold cooked fish, finely chopped, seasoned, plus a little lemon juice or cream.

Fruit Kebabs

A wonderful way to serve a quick fruity breakfast.

small cubes ham
pineapple chunks
small apples, cored, thickly sliced
oranges, cut into segments with skin intact
bananas, thickly sliced
melted butter

Thread ham with the fruit alternately onto skewers. Brush with melted butter and grill to heat through. Remove from skewers and serve with cottage cheese.

Hearty Vegetable Casserole

A good vegetarian lunch recipe.
2 carrots, sliced
250g (8oz) trimmed broccoli
4 small potatoes, sliced
½ medium onion, finely chopped
2 tablespoons water
2 medium zucchini, sliced
1 x 440g (15oz) can*, cream of chicken soup
1 cup sweet corn kernels
1 cup grated tasty cheese
2 teaspoons caraway seeds
½ cup breadcrumbs
1 egg, beaten

*Nearest equivalent can size.

Place the carrots, broccoli, potatoes and onion with the water into the base of a 5 cup casserole. Cover and microwave on HIGH for 8 minutes. Add the zucchini and microwave for a further 2 minutes. Combine the soup, corn, cheese, caraway seeds, breadcrumbs and beaten egg, in a large bowl. Drain the vegetables and add to the soup mixture. Cover and microwave on HIGH for 4 minutes. Allow to stand 3 minutes before serving.
Serves 4.

Quick Tuna Asparagus Bake

Serve as a quick snack on muffins, toast or with rice or noodles.
1 x 440g (15oz) can* cream asparagus soup
1 x 425g (13oz) can* tuna, drained, flaked
3 hard boiled eggs, quartered
1 x 280g (9oz) can* champignons, drained
1 cup frozen peas
1 cup potato chips, lightly crushed

*Nearest equivalent can size.

Combine all ingredients with the exception of the potato chips in a 5 cup casserole. Top with the chips. Cover and microwave on MEDIUM-HIGH for 5 minutes
Serves 4-5.

Photograph opposite:
Commonwealth Gardens, Canberra, A.C.T.

Photograph below:
"Willoura" Station, New South Wales.

Paw Paw and Mango Beef Olives

For those who love meat and fruit combinations, this makes an excellent main course, and can be served hot with the sauce or cold with the accompanying fruit.

6 thinly sliced pieces topside steak
1 x 175g (6oz) jar paw paw and mango chutney
2 cups wholemeal fresh breadcrumbs
½ teaspoon oregano
½ teaspoon marjoram
seasoning to taste
60g (2oz) butter or margarine
1 onion, finely chopped
1 shallot, finely sliced
1 tablespoon oil
The Sauce:
2 tablespoons tomato paste
2 tablespoons cornflour
1 x 440g (15oz) can* beef consomme

*Nearest equivalent can size.

Place steaks on a chopping board and pound, using a meat mallet. Spread with ⅔ of the paw paw and mango chutney. Combine breadcrumbs, herbs and seasoning in a bowl. Melt the butter in the microwave on HIGH for 1½ minutes. Add the onion and shallot and microwave on HIGH for 2 minutes, then stir into the breadcrumb mixture. Sprinkle over the steaks and chutney, roll up and secure with toothpicks. Brush with oil and place in a shallow dish. Cover and microwave on HIGH for 6 minutes, turning occasionally, then on MEDIUM-HIGH for 4 minutes. Allow to stand. Combine the tomato paste, cornflour and remaining chutney in a 4 cup bowl and gradually mix in the beef consommé. Microwave on HIGH for 6 minutes, stirring 2-3 times during cooking. Pour over the beef, cover and microwave on MEDIUM for 6-8 minutes. Remove toothpicks and serve with pineapple wedges and fresh paw paw or mango.
Serves 6.

Photograph above:
"Old Melbourne Inn", Melbourne, Victoria.

Photograph page 250/251:
Jenolan Caves, New South Wales.

Chicken and Bacon Casserole

An ideal recipe for an informal dinner, as it can be prepared ahead of time and reheated in the microwave if wished.

60g (2oz) butter or margarine
2 tablespoons oil
seasoned flour
1.5kg (3lb) chicken pieces
4 sticks celery, sliced
2 large onions, sliced
125g (4oz) mushrooms, sliced
4 rashers bacon, roughly chopped
2 cloves garlic, crushed
3 tablespoons flour
2½ cups chicken stock
seasoning to taste
⅓ cup parsley sprigs

Melt the butter in the oil, using a large saucepan, and sauté the lightly floured chicken pieces on both sides until golden brown. Remove from pan. Add celery, onions, mushrooms, bacon and garlic and cook for approximately 2 minutes. Add flour, stir for 1 minute, then add the stock and seasoning. Stir until sauce boils and thickens. Place chicken into an ovenproof casserole, pour the sauce over and bake, covered, at 180°C (350°F) for 40 minutes or until chicken is tender. Sprinkle with chopped parsley and serve.
Serves 4-6.

Tasty Hamburgers

(Photograph opposite)

These hamburgers could be served in pita bread with shredded lettuce, tomato, cucumber and perhaps a fried egg on top.

500g (1lb) minced steak
1 onion, finely chopped
½ cup dried breadcrumbs
1 egg, lightly beaten
1 tablespoon tomato sauce
1 tablespoon Parmesan cheese
1 teaspoon Worcestershire sauce
1 tablespoon evaporated milk
1 tablespoon lemon juice
2 tablespoons chopped parsley
seasoning to taste
1-2 tablespoons oil

Combine the ingredients, with the exception of the oil, and form into hamburgers, allowing 2 tablespoons per serve. Heat the oil in a dish in the microwave for approximately 5 minutes on HIGH. Add the hamburgers. Cover and microwave for 12-15 minutes on HIGH. Allow to stand 3-4 minutes, then serve with your favourite sauce.
Serves 6-8.

Lamb Curry with Fruit

(Photograph this page)

Serve with fluffy rice and sauteed mixed blanched nuts, papadams, and a plate of fresh fruits such as paw paw, sliced banana, apple wedges and pineapple.

500g (1lb) lean lamb, cubed
2 tablespoons seasoned flour
2 cloves garlic, crushed
1 onion, chopped
1 stick celery, sliced
2 tablespoons oil
1 tablespoon curry powder
2 tablespoons fruit chutney
1-1½ cups beef stock
1 teaspoon lemon juice
½ green apple, diced
¼ cup sultanas

Toss meat in the flour and set aside. Microwave the vegetables in the oil on HIGH for 3 minutes, add curry powder and microwave for a further 2 minutes on HIGH. Stir in the lamb and add the beef stock. Cover and microwave on HIGH for 10 minutes, then stir in the sultanas, lemon juice and apple. Microwave on MEDIUM-HIGH for 10 minutes, stir and microwave for a further 10 minutes. Serves 4.

Photograph opposite:
(Recipe this page)
Tasty Hot Dog and Bean Salad

Photograph below:
(Recipe this page)
Lamb Curry with Fruit

Tomato Glazed Meat Loaf

Meat loaf makes an excellent, economical buffet or luncheon dish. Leftovers can be thinly sliced and used as a sandwich filling.

750g (1½lb) minced steak
⅔ cup dried breadcrumbs
150 ml (¼ pint) evaporated milk
1 egg
1 onion, finely chopped
2 tablespoons tomato sauce
1 tablespoon Worcestershire sauce
½ teaspoon mustard
2 beef stock cubes, crumbled
seasoning to taste
The glaze:
¼ cup tomato sauce
1 tablespoon brown sugar
1 teaspoon mustard

Combine all the ingredients for the meat loaf and press into a loaf dish. Cover and microwave on HIGH for 10 minutes. Drain off fat and excess juices and continue to microwave, uncovered, a further 5 minutes on MEDIUM-HIGH, allow to stand. Combine the ingredients for the glaze in a small bowl and microwave for 4 minutes on MEDIUM-HIGH. Turn meat loaf out onto a serving dish and brush with the glaze, return to the microwave and cook on HIGH for 2 minutes. Serve hot or cold with fresh vegetables and a garnish of fresh herbs.
Serves 6-8.

Swedish Meatballs

As an alternative, these meatballs may be served with whole boiled potatoes, or buttered noodles and tomato chutney.

3 slices bread, crusts removed
1 egg, beaten
½ cup water
60g (2oz) butter or margarine
1 large onion, finely diced
750g (1½ lb) minced beef
seasoning to taste
3 tablespoons cornflour
1½ cups water
⅔ cup evaporated milk
1 teaspoon soy sauce

Soak the bread in the combined egg and water. Melt half the butter with the onion in a container and microwave on HIGH for 3 minutes. Stir into the bread mixture. Add the mince, season and form into approximately 36 balls. Cook in 3 batches on HIGH allowing approximately 10 minutes each batch, then transfer to a deep 9 cup casserole. Prepare the sauce by melting the remaining butter in a container, on HIGH for 1 minute. Add cornflour and combine until smooth. Microwave for a further 1 minute on HIGH. Gradually stir in water, microwave on HIGH for 3 minutes, stirring frequently during cooking. Add evaporated milk, soy sauce and seasoning, stir and pour over meatballs. Cover and cook on MEDIUM for approximately 12-15 minutes. Serve hot, sprinkled with paprika and chopped parsley.
Serves 4-6.

Hot Dogs

(Photograph opposite)

Everyone loves a hot dog and those served straight from the microwave will certainly be a family favourite.

4 frankfurters
2 tablespoons water
4 hot dog rolls
mustard or tomato sauce

Pierce the frankfurters with a skewer or sharp knife and place in a shallow casserole. Add water, cover and microwave on MEDIUM for 3½ minutes. Allow to stand. Warm the rolls on HIGH for 30 seconds. Split, and fill with the frankfurters with your choice of mustard or sauce.
Serves 4.

Tomato and Mushroom Bake

For a crispy brown topping, place under a conventional preheated grill for 3-4 minutes or until browned.

30g (1oz) butter or margarine
1 onion, sliced
1 shallot, chopped
500g (1lb) ripe tomatoes, sliced
½ cup sliced mushrooms
seasoning to taste
mixed herbs
½ teaspoon raw sugar
¾ cup wholemeal breadcrumbs
¼ cup Parmesan cheese

Place half the butter in a 4 cup casserole with the onion and shallot and microwave on HIGH for 2 minutes. Add tomatoes, mushrooms, seasoning and herbs. Sprinkle with sugar, breadcrumbs and Parmesan cheese. Dot with the remaining butter, cover, and microwave on HIGH for 6 minutes.
Serves 3-4.

Glazed Ham Steaks

2 tablespoons brown sugar
2 tablespoons pineapple juice
6 cloves
1 teaspoon French mustard
1 teaspoon Worcestershire sauce
4 ham steaks
4 slices pineapple

Place sugar, juice, cloves, mustard and sauce in a small bowl and microwave on HIGH for 4 minutes, to create a thick, syrupy sauce. Arrange ham steaks in a square baking dish with a slice of pineapple on each one. Glaze with the sauce and microwave on MEDIUM-HIGH for 5 minutes.
Serves 4.

Honeyed Chicken Wings
(Photograph page 268/269)

These delicious wings can be served hot or at room temperature. They are very versatile and can be served as a main course, entree or as an excellent picnic food.

2 tablespoons peanut oil
⅓ cup soy sauce
2 tablespoons honey
2 tablespoons dry sherry
1 clove garlic, crushed
2 teaspoons Hoi Sin sauce
½ teaspoon finely grated root ginger
20 chicken wings

Make the marinade by combining the first seven ingredients. Place chicken wings in a large baking dish and pour over the marinade. Marinate for 2 hours, turning occasionally. Cover and microwave on HIGH for 6 minutes. Turn over wings and move centre ones to outside of dish. Microwave a further 6 minutes on MEDIUM-HIGH. Stand for 5 minutes before serving.
Serves 6-8.

Speedy Chow Mein
(Photograph page 257)

This speedy Chow Mein is delicious served with crusty bread or toast and garnished with spring onions.

500g (1lb) minced steak
1 onion, finely chopped
1 cup cooked rice
2½ cups water
1 packet chicken noodle soup
1 tablespoon curry powder
4 cups finely shredded cabbage
1 x 440g (15oz) can* pineapple pieces, drained
¼ cup chopped chives

*Nearest equivalent can size.

Combine all ingredients, with the exception of the cabbage, pineapple and chives, in a 9 cup casserole. Stir thoroughly, cover and microwave on HIGH for 10 minutes. Add the cabbage and pineapple, combine thoroughly, then microwave on MEDIUM-HIGH for a further 8 minutes.
Serves 5-6.

Photograph opposite page:
The Strand Arcade, Sydney, New South Wales.

Photograph opposite:
"Henley on Todd Regatta", Alice Springs, Northern Territory.

Photograph page 254/255:
Paddle riverboat "Melbourne" on the Murray River, Mildura District, Victoria.

COOKING FROM AROUND THE WORLD

Although Australia is still a young country, in comparison with its European and Asian neighbours, it is a rapidly growing cosmopolitan country and therefore open to the world's culinary delights.

We have many thousands of first generation Italians, Greeks, Chinese, Yugoslavs, Germans, Dutch, Maltese, Polish, Turkish, Hungarians, Russians, and many more different nationalities. The enormous influence of this multi-national population is evident in our fine restaurants, delicatessens, take-away food bars, supermarkets and patisseries. It is also evident in the fact that Australians are learning to experiment with international cooking and constantly broadening their repertoire of recipes to contain exotic foreign delicacies.

We have meat, dairy foods, fruit, vegetables and aromatic spices readily available – in fact any food or ingredient imaginable, can be purchased in our cosmopolitan country. Many international dishes have become a permanent part of our weekly menus.

This chapter brings you a variety of our favourite international recipes.

Photograph opposite:
Moussaka (Recipe page 273)

Photograph page 272:
Left: Minestrone Soup
(Recipe page 21)
Right: Chicken and Oatmeal Soup
(Recipe page 274)

Moussaka

Moussaka often referred to as the cottage pie of the Balkans, has many versions, but usually consists of layers of seasonal vegetables alternating with layers of minced meat.

4 small eggplant, halved
250g. (8oz) lamb, cubed, fat removed
1 medium onion, quartered
1 clove garlic
oil for frying
2 tomatoes, quartered
1 tablespoon tomato paste
1 teaspoon sugar
few drops Tabasco sauce
seasoning to taste
1 egg
tomato sauce
½ cup grated cheese

Sprinkle egg plant with salt, leave for 15 minutes, then rinse and pat dry. Mince the lamb with the onion and garlic. Heat the oil in a frying pan, add meat and saute until well browned. Puree the tomatoes with the tomato paste, sugar, Tabasco sauce, and seasoning. Heat oil and shallow fry eggplant, flesh side down until golden brown. Drain on paper towelling. With a spoon, scoop out flesh and combine with the meat mixture and the egg, mixing well together. Spoon into shells and arrange in a greased ovenproof dish, top with a small quantity of tomato sauce. Sprinkle with grated cheese and bake at 180°C (350°F) for 30 minutes.
Serves 8 as an entree
or 4 as a main meal.

Borsch

A rich red wine coloured soup, made from beetroot, is the basic soup of Russia and Poland, and always served with sour cream.

10 cups beef stock
4 beetroot, peeled, sliced
2 potatoes, finely chopped
1 large onion, finely chopped
1 clove garlic, crushed
1 tablespoon lemon juice
freshly ground pepper
sour cream
chopped chives

Bring stock to the boil, add prepared vegetables and simmer 45 minutes or until beetroot is tender. Add lemon juice and pepper. Serve soup topped with a spoonful of sour cream and chives.
Serves 6-8.

Spinach and Feta Triangles

2 tablespoons butter or margarine
1 x 250g (8oz) packet frozen spinach, thawed
3 onions, finely chopped
¼ cup finely chopped shallots
3 eggs, beaten
250g (8oz) Feta cheese, chopped
2 teaspoons nutmeg
seasoning to taste
15 sheets filo pastry
125g (4oz) butter or margarine, melted

Melt butter, sauté spinach, onions and shallots, remove from the heat. Add eggs, cheese, nutmeg, and seasoning, beating well until combined. Divide pastry in half, lengthwise, then fold each sheet again in half, lengthwise and brush with butter. Place a tablespoon of filling on end of strip of pastry. Fold corner of pastry over filling to form a triangle. Continue to fold pastry over in triangles to the end. Repeat with remaining pastry and filling. Place onto a baking sheet, brush with butter and bake at 190°C (375°F) for 20-25 minutes, or until cooked. Makes 15 triangles.

Brodetta

(Photograph this page)
Brodetta also makes a very good accompaniment to the Australian barbeque.

3 tomatoes, sliced

The Sauce:

2 tablespoons cornflour
2 cups milk
1 tablespoon chopped basil
90g (3oz) grated tasty cheese
1 cup breadcrumbs

Grease a shallow ovenproof baking dish and arrange tomato slices over the base. Blend cornflour with a little milk, pour into a saucepan with the remaining milk, and basil. Bring to the boil and cook for 1 minute stirring constantly. Remove from the heat and add ¾ of the cheese. Pour over the tomatoes and sprinkle with breadcrumbs. Top with remaining cheese and bake at 200°C (400°F) for 10 minutes or until heated through and browned.
Serves 3.

*Photograph below:
Brodetta*

Gazpacho

Gazpacho is known, as far back as Greek and Roman literature where it is mentioned as a "drinkable food". The name Gazpacho is derived from the Arabic for "soaked bread". Gazpacho is made all over Spain, with different regions using a variety of foods for the base.

1 cucumber, peeled, seeded, chopped
4 tomatoes, skinned, chopped
2 onions, chopped
1 green capsicum, chopped
2 cloves garlic, crushed
3 cups water
4 tablespoons red wine vinegar
2 teaspoons salt
2 tablespoons olive oil
2 cups bread crumbs, crust removed

Garnishes:

chopped cucumber, onions, capsicum and hard-boiled egg

Combine ingredients in a food processor until smooth. Refrigerate for 2 hours and serve with garnishes. Serves 4.

Chicken & Oatmeal Soup

(Photograph page 272)
1 small chicken
8 cups chicken stock
2 carrots, roughly chopped
1 parsnip, roughly chopped
2 onions, roughly chopped
2 sticks celery, sliced
¼ cup chopped parsley
seasoning to taste
1 packet chicken noodle soup
¼ cup coarse oatmeal

Place the chicken in a saucepan with the stock and simmer over a low heat for 2-3 hours. Transfer to a bowl, allow to cool and refrigerate overnight. Skim off fat, remove skin and bone from chicken, and chop the flesh. Place the jellied stock, and chicken with all the remaining ingredients in a large saucepan and simmer until the vegetables are tender, approximately 1 hour. Serve in deep soup bowls with crusty bread.
Serves 10.

French Onion Soup

30g (1oz) butter or margarine
6 onions, sliced
6 cups beef stock
430g (14oz) can* beef consommé
pepper to taste
½ cup grated cheese
*Nearest equivalent can size.

Melt butter in a saucepan, add onions and cook over a medium heat until tender and lightly browned. Add stock, beef consommé and pepper. Bring to the boil and simmer for 20 minutes. Serve hot, sprinkled with cheese. Serves 6-8.

Photograph opposite:
Noodle maker at work.

Photograph below:
Enjoying a meal at a Teppan Yaki Bar.
Suntory Restaurant, Sydney, New South Wales.

Dim Sims

(Photograph this page)

125g (4oz) minced pork
4 shallots, finely chopped
1 cup shredded cabbage
10 shelled prawns, finely chopped
1 tablespoon cornflour
1 egg
2 tablespoons soy sauce
few drops sesame oil
¼ teaspoon salt
wanton wrappers
oil for frying

Combine all chopped ingredients, with cornflour, egg, soy sauce, sesame oil and salt mixing well. Place a teaspoon of mixture into centre of each wanton wrapper, pinch the wanton skin together at the top to form a small package. Heat oil and deep fry until golden brown. Drain and serve with soy sauce or sweet and sour sauce.
Makes approximately 30.

Spring Rolls

(Photograph this page)

A small stuffed pancake, belonging to Chinese cooking. There are many varieties of fillings which range from chicken, fish, pork etc., but they are extremely popular not only in South-East Asia but Australia also.

250g (8oz) pork mince
¼ small cabbage, shredded
6 shallots, finely chopped
1 stick celery, finely chopped
¼ cup water chestnuts
2 tablespoons soy sauce
1 teaspoon salt
1 teaspoon sugar
pepper
1 tablespoon cornflour
¼ cup water
250g (8oz) packet spring roll wrappers
oil for frying

Combine pork with vegetables, water chestnuts, soy sauce, salt, sugar and pepper mixing well. Combine cornflour and water, stirring till smooth. Spread approximately 2 tablespoons of pork mixture evenly across the corner of the spring roll wrapper. Brush edges with cornflour mixture and roll up in an envelope shape, making sure edges are well sealed. Heat oil and deep fry spring rolls a few at a time until golden brown and cooked through. Drain on absorbent paper and serve.
Makes 20.

Chinese Beef

3 tablespoons oil
1 kg (2lb) rump, partially frozen, sliced
1 onion, sliced
4 sticks celery, sliced
6 shallots, chopped
230g (7oz) can* whole bamboo
shoots, drained, sliced
1 red capsicum, seeded, sliced
3 cloves garlic, crushed
1 small nob root ginger, sliced
2 cups beef stock
2 tablespoons soy sauce
2 tablespoons sweet sherry
1½ tablespoons sugar
seasoning to taste
6 spinach leaves
3 tablespoons cornflour

*Nearest equivalent can size.

Heat oil in a wok or frying pan and
stir-fry ½ the meat until well
browned. Remove from the pan and
stir-fry the remaining meat. Add all
sliced vegetables and meat to the
pan and stir fry for a further 2
minutes. Add stock, soy sauce,
sherry, sugar, seasoning and spinach
leaves torn into pieces. Mix
cornflour with sufficient water to
make a smooth paste and add to
meat and vegetables, stirring well
until mixture boils and thickens.
Simmer approximately 5 minutes or
until meat and spinach leaves are
tender. Serve with rice.
Serves 4-6.

Photograph above:
(Recipes this page)
Left: Spring Rolls
Right: Dim Sims

Photograph page 279:
A Latvian beauty wearing traditional
dancing dress.

Photograph page 282/283:
"Chinatown By Night", Sydney, New South Wales.

Photograph page 284:
Chicken and Sausage Gumbo
(Recipe page 285)

Photograph page 285:
"Vintage Queens", Barossa Valley Wine Festival,
South Australia.

Photograph page 286/287:
"Harry's Cafe de Wheels",
world famous for Pies 'n' Peas,
Sydney, New South Wales.

Oriental Fish with Pineapple Sauce

1 tablespoon oil
1 red capsicum, seeded, sliced
3 medium carrots, sliced
½ cucumber, sliced
2 medium onions, sliced
1 small pineapple, peeled, cored, sliced
2 tablespoons cornflour
4 tablespoons vinegar
2 tablespoons sugar
1 tablespoon soy sauce
1 cup chicken stock
2 tablespoons sherry
4 medium snapper
soy sauce
cornflour for coating
oil for frying

Heat the oil in a saucepan. Add the vegetables and pineapple and cook for 3 minutes. Stir in cornflour, vinegar, sugar, soy sauce, stock and sherry. Bring to boil, stirring continuously until sauce thickens. Simmer 3 minutes. Score the fish on both sides diagonally with a knife. Rub with soy sauce, coat lightly in cornflour, shake off excess. Pan fry fish in a small quantity of oil until well browned and cooked on both sides. Serve hot with pineapple sauce.
Serves 4.

Pizza

The word Pizza means pie in Italian, and is usually made in the form of a round of yeast dough spread with tomatoes and Mozzarella cheese and baked in a hot oven. There are many varieties, but try this tasty one below.

The Base:
1½ cups flour
½ teaspoon salt
1 teaspoon sugar
1 sachet dried yeast
½ cup luke warm water
3 tablespoons oil
1 cup Tomato and Garlic Sauce (see recipe this page)
250g (8oz) Mozzarella cheese, grated
2 tablespoons grated Parmesan cheese

The Topping:
prawns
anchovies
pepperoni slices
strips of capsicum
chopped onions
chopped bacon
sliced mushrooms

Sift flour into a large bowl and mix in salt, sugar and yeast. Pour water and oil into centre of dry ingredients and mix to form a dough. Turn onto a lightly floured board and knead until smooth and elastic. Cover dough and stand in a warm place to double in size for approximately 30-40 minutes. Roll dough out to fit a 25cm (10") oiled pizza plate. Spread sauce over dough, sprinkle with topping ingredients, ending with the cheese. Allow pizza to stand again in a warm place for 15 minutes. Bake at 230°C (450°F) for 15-20 minutes.

Risotto

An Italian dish of rice, usually made with thick short grained Italian rice, flavoured with numerous vegetables and served generously with Parmesan cheese.

1½ tablespoons butter or margarine
2 onions, chopped
1 cup cooked rice
1 cup sliced mushrooms
2 cups chicken stock
1½ cups white wine
1 clove garlic, crushed
pinch saffron
seasoning to taste
1 bay leaf
3 tablespoons Parmesan cheese
1 tablespoon butter or margarine

Melt the butter and saute onion until tender. Stir in rice and cook for 2-3 minutes. Add mushrooms, saute lightly. Add the stock, 1 cup of wine, the garlic, saffron, seasoning and bay leaf. Simmer until rice is tender, stirring occasionally and adding the remaining wine as the rice absorbs the liquid. When rice is tender, remove from heat and adjust seasonings. Sprinkle with Parmesan cheese, dot with butter, cover pan and leave for 5 minutes. Stir lightly and serve.
Serves 4.

Tomato and Garlic Sauce

1 tablespoon oil
2 onions, finely chopped
3 cloves garlic, crushed
1 x 475g (16oz) can tomatoes, coarsely chopped
¼ cup tomato paste
¼ cup red wine
1 teaspoon oregano
½ teaspoon basil
1 bay leaf
2 teaspoons sugar
seasoning to taste

Heat oil and saute onion until tender. Add garlic and cook for 1-2 minutes. Add tomatoes with their liquid and remaining sauce ingredients. Bring to the boil and then simmer uncovered for 1 hour, stirring occasionally. Remove bay leaf and adjust seasonings to taste. The sauce should be smooth and thick when cooked. When cool, sauce can be kept in refrigerator until required.

Chicken & Ham Cannelloni

(Photograph this page)

Cannelloni are numbered among the largest of the stuffed paste of Italy. Usually squares of pasta cooked, then stuffed with a savoury filling rolled up and browned in the oven.

The Filling:

250g (8oz) minced chicken
125g (4oz) ham, minced
¼ cup chopped parsley
4 shallots, chopped
2 sticks celery, sliced
seasoning to taste
1 egg

The Tomato Sauce:

1 x 440g (14oz) can* tomatoes
2 cloves garlic, crushed
½ teaspoon basil
seasoning to taste
1 teaspoon sugar

The Cheese Sauce:

60g (2oz) butter or margarine
3 tablespoons flour
2 cups milk
½ cup cream
¾ cup grated cheese

For Cooking:

15 cannelloni shells, pre-cooked
*Nearest equivalent can size.

Combine all the filling ingredients together in a bowl. Make the tomato sauce by pureeing the undrained tomatoes with garlic. Transfer to a saucepan, add the seasonings and sugar, and simmer uncovered for 10 minutes. Make the cheese sauce by melting the butter in a saucepan, add the flour, and cook for 1 minute, gradually add milk and stir until sauce boils and thickens. Stir in cream and ½ of the cheese. Stir ½ cup of cheese sauce into the chicken filling and use to fill the cannelloni shells. Spoon a thin layer of tomato sauce over the base of a greased ovenproof dish, large enough to take the cannelloni in a single layer. Place cannelloni in dish and cover completely with the remaining cheese sauce. Top with the tomato sauce and sprinkle with the grated cheese. Bake at 180°C (350°F) for 40 minutes.
Serves 6.

Braised Fennel

A delicious vegetable, and delicately flavoured with anisette. It is used both as a herb and a vegetable, and often served as an excellent accompaniment to fish.

4 fennel bulbs, quartered
2 tablespoons olive oil
1 clove garlic, crushed
freshly ground black pepper
2 tablespoons tomato paste
1 cup white wine

Wash and drain fennel and sauté in the oil with the garlic, approximately 10 minutes. Season. Blend the tomato paste with the wine and pour over the fennel. Cover and simmer 15 minutes or until tender.
Serves 4.

Scallops Cacciatore

(Photograph this page)
500g (1lb) scallops
¼ cup lemon juice
1 cup tomato puree
1 clove garlic, crushed
1 teaspoon salt
4 peppercorns
1 tablespoon wine vinegar
¼ cup finely chopped onion
1 capsicum, finely sliced
½ cup mushrooms, finely sliced

Place the scallops in an ovenproof dish, with the lemon juice and bake at 180°C (350°F) for 5 minutes. Combine all the remaining ingredients in a saucepan and bring to the boil. Reduce heat and simmer for 5 minutes. Pour the sauce over the scallops, return to the oven and cook a further 15 minutes.

Italian Meat Balls

500g (1lb) beef, veal or pork, minced
2 rashers bacon, chopped
1 onion, finely chopped
1 egg
pinch oregano
pinch nutmeg
seasoning to taste
1 cup fresh breadcrumbs
2½ cups stock
1 tablespoon seasoned flour
oil for frying
cooked pasta
Tomato and Garlic Sauce (see recipe page 278)

Combine the meat, bacon and onion with the egg, oregano, nutmeg, seasoning and breadcrumbs. Mould into small balls, adding a little stock if mixture is too dry. Toss in seasoned flour and fry in hot oil until golden brown. Remove and poach in the heated stock for approximately 10-15 minutes. Drain and serve with pasta and Tomato and Garlic Sauce.
Serves 4.

Variations: Add finely grated Parmesan cheese to meat mixture. Add a few finely chopped or minced anchovies to meat mixture.

Photograph below:
Scallops Cacciatore
(Recipe this page)

Photograph opposite:
Chicken and Ham Canneloni
(Recipe this page)

Quiche Lorraine

The most famous of all Quiches with its filling of eggs, cream and bacon.

Rich Short Crust Pastry.

2 cups flour
pinch salt
150g (5oz) butter or margarine
1 egg yolk
squeeze lemon juice
2 tablespoons water

The Filling:

3 rashers bacon, chopped
125g (4oz) Gruyere cheese, grated
3 eggs
1 cup cream
pepper, nutmeg to taste
½ teaspoon dry mustard

Make the pastry by sifting the flour and salt together into a bowl. Rub in the butter. Beat the egg yolk, lemon juice and water together and add to the dry ingredients to make a firm dough. Wrap and chill for 30 minutes. Roll out the pastry and line a 20cm (8") quiche dish. Bake "blind" at 220°C (440°F) for 10 minutes. Remove paper and bake for a further 3 minutes. Allow to cool. Cook bacon until crisp and drain. Sprinkle over pastry base and top with grated cheese. Combine eggs, cream, and seasonings and carefully pour into the pastry case. Bake at 190°C (375°F) for 45 minutes or until golden brown.
Serves 6-8.

Beef Bourguignon

A traditional French dish, flavoured with good wine, and has a wonderful aroma.

2 cups red wine
1 carrot, sliced
2 onions, sliced
½ cup chopped parsley
2 cloves garlic, crushed
2 tablespoons oil
1 bay leaf
pinch thyme
seasoning to taste
1½kg (3lb) chuck or round steak, cubed
2 tablespoons butter or margarine
1 tablespoon flour
½ cup consommé
24 small white onions
125g (4oz) salt pork, diced
1½ cups sliced mushrooms

Combine wine, carrot, onions, parsley, garlic, oil and seasonings in a deep bowl. Add the beef and marinate for 4 hours, turning the meat occasionally. Remove the meat and drain well on paper towelling. Strain the marinade and set aside. Heat the butter in a large frying pan. Add the meat and brown well on all sides. Add the flour, stir and cook for 2 minutes, then stir in the consommé and reserved marinade. Cover and bring to the boil. Lower heat and simmer, covered for 2 hours. Sauté onions and salt pork for 10 minutes or until brown. Pour off the fat and add the pork and onions to the meat mixture, with the mushrooms. Cover and simmer for 45 minutes or until meat is tender.
Serves 6-8.

Sauerkraut

A method of preserving cabbage for the people of northern Europe, who were snow-bound during the winter months.

2 onions, chopped
2 tablespoons pork fat
2 x 430g (14oz) cans* sauerkraut, drained
2 cups apples, peeled, sliced
1 x 430g (14oz) can* beef consommé
2 tablespoons vinegar
1 tablespoon flour
2 tablespoons water
1 potato, grated
pinch caraway seeds
*Nearest equivalent can size.

Sauté onion in a large frying pan with the pork fat until golden. Add sauerkraut, apples, consommé and vinegar and simmer uncovered for 15 minutes. Blend flour with water until smooth, then stir into the sauerkraut with the potato and caraway seeds. Cook over moderate heat, stirring until slightly thickened and potato has cooked.
Serves 4-6.

Fish Veronique

4 shallots, finely chopped
1kg (2lb) fish fillets
1 cup white wine
seasoning to taste
1 tablespoon butter or margarine
2 tablespoons flour
3 tablespoons grape juice
1 cup cream
1 x 250g (8oz) can seedless white grapes

Grease an ovenproof casserole dish and sprinkle with the shallots. Arrange fish on top and pour over the wine. Season and bake at 180°C (350°F) for 12-15 minutes or until fish is tender. Transfer to a serving dish and keep warm. Strain liquid from casserole into a saucepan and reduce by half. Melt the butter in a saucepan, add flour and cook for 1 minute. Add the grape juice to the fish stock and stir into the roux to make a smooth sauce. Simmer gently for 7 minutes. Add cream, reheat but do not boil. Add grapes and spoon over fish. Serve hot, garnished with lemon and parsley.
Serves 6-8.

Sauerbraten

One of Germany's most celebrated dishes, and an excellent way of tenderising tough meat.

1½kg (3lb) piece fresh silverside
1 cup water
1 cup vinegar
2 tablespoons brown sugar
seasoning to taste
8 peppercorns
2 cloves
1 bay leaf
2 cloves garlic, crushed
1 tablespoon butter or margarine
2 onions, chopped
1 carrot, diced
2 tablespoons chopped parsley
1 tablespoon flour
½ cup sour cream

Place meat in a bowl with the water, vinegar, brown sugar, seasoning, peppercorns, cloves, bay leaf and garlic. Cover and leave in refrigerator for 3-4 days, turning meat daily. Remove meat from marinade, drain well and pat dry. Reserve marinade. Melt butter and brown meat on all sides. Add half marinade with onions, carrot and parsley. Cover and bring to the boil. Simmer gently for 2½ hours. Blend extra flour with a little water and add to liquid, bring to the boil and simmer for 2 minutes, stirring constantly. Add sour cream, check seasoning and strain into a sauce boat. Serve with meat.
Serves 6-8.

Tabouleh

A very popular dish from the Middle East. The burghul gives a delicious nutty flavour, and the dish is excellent served with pita bread.

½ cup burghul (cracked wheat)
1½ cups chopped tomatoes
¾ cup finely chopped shallots
1½ cups chopped parsley
1 teaspoon salt
⅓ cup olive oil
⅓ cup lemon juice
2 tablespoons chopped fresh mint

Soak burghul in luke warm water for 1 hour. Drain and spread on paper towel to dry. Combine burghul with tomatoes, shallots, parsley and salt. Whisk together oil, lemon juice and mint and combine the two mixtures. Refrigerate until well chilled and serve on a bed of lettuce.
Serves 4.

Chicken and Sausage Gumbo

(Photograph page 284)
This is a traditional Creole dish and is a cross between a stew and a soup.

½ cup vegetable oil
1 chicken, jointed
⅓ cup flour
6 cups cold water
500g (1lb) Polish or French garlic smoked sausage, sliced
250g (8oz) lean ham steaks, cubed
2 cups chopped onions
½ cup chopped capsicum
½ cup chopped shallots
2 tablespoons chopped parsley
2 cloves garlic, crushed
1 teaspoon dried thyme
3 whole bay leaves, crumbled
seasoning to taste

Heat oil in a large saucepan and brown the chicken pieces. Remove from pan, stir in the flour and cook until lightly browned. Gradually add a little water to make a gravy. Add sausage, ham and vegetables and continue cooking until tender. Return chicken to the pan with remaining water, herbs and seasoning. Cover and simmer for approximately 1 hour or until chicken and vegetables are tender. Serve in deep bowls over cooked rice.
Serves 6-8.

Chilli Con Carne

Traditionally a Mexican dish of beef in a chilli sauce, but now popular throughout the world. Usually a very hot spicy dish, but one can vary the amount of chillies.

1kg (2lb) minced steak
2 onions, finely chopped
2 cloves garlic, crushed
3 tablespoons oil
500g (1lb) tomatoes, pureed
1 cup beef stock
3 tablespoons tomato paste
2 teaspoons — 2 tablespoons chilli powder or to taste
1 teaspoon cumin
¼ teaspoon oregano
seasoning to taste
1 x 450g (15oz) can* red kidney beans, drained
*Nearest equivalent can size.

Combine meat with onions and garlic. Heat oil in a frying pan and sauté meat over a high heat until well browned. Add tomatoes, stock, tomato paste and seasonings. Bring to the boil, reduce heat and simmer, covered for 30 minutes. Rinse beans, drain and add to the meat mixture. Simmer, covered for a further 30 minutes.
Serves 4-6.

Tacos with Chilli Beef

(Photograph this page)
This is probably one of the most popular Mexican recipes and is a natural inclusion in this section. Use also, as a filling for Pita bread.

500g (1lb) minced steak
1 onion, finely chopped
1 clove garlic, crushed
1½ tablespoons oil
250g (8oz) tomatoes, pureed
½ cup beef stock
2 tablespoons tomato paste
1 teaspoon chilli powder
½ teaspoon cumin
seasoning to taste
1 packet taco shells
¾ cup grated cheese
2 tomatoes, roughly chopped
4 lettuce leaves, shredded
1 onion roughly chopped

Combine meat with onion and garlic. Heat oil in a frying pan and sauté meat over a high heat until meat is well browned. Add tomatoes, stock, tomato paste and seasonings. Bring to the boil, reduce heat and simmer, covered, for 30 minutes. Place taco shells onto a baking sheet and heat through in the oven at 180°C (350°F) for 5 minutes. Spoon some grated cheese into taco shells, top with meat, tomatoes, lettuce and onion.
Serves 6.

Hot Meat Curry

Curries may vary from meat, chicken to vegetables, and may range from mild to extremely hot, but served with the correct accompaniments they are something we can all enjoy.

1kg (2lb) lean lamb or mutton chops
4 dried chillies
2 tablespoons ghee or clarified butter
1 small nob root ginger, finely chopped
3 cloves garlic, crushed
3 large onions, chopped
2 tablespoons curry powder
1 cup water
seasoning to taste
lemon juice
cooked rice

Trim and cut meat into small cubes. Soak the chillies in a little hot water for 5 minutes. Strain, then chop finely, removing the seeds. Heat the ghee and sauté the meat with the ginger and garlic. Reduce heat, add the onions, curry powder, chillies and water. Cover and simmer for about 2 hours. Season and add lemon juice to taste. Serve with hot cooked rice and a selection of the following accompaniments:- chutney, sliced bananas, apples or tomatoes, dried fruits, peanuts or cashews, cucumber, coconut.
Serves 4-6.

Curried Rice Croquettes

60g (2oz) butter or margarine
1 onion, finely chopped
¼ cup flour
1 tablespoon curry powder
1 cup milk
½ teaspoon salt
pinch cayenne pepper
2 cups cooked brown rice
1½ cups minced steak, cooked
seasoned flour
1 egg
1 tablespoon water
dried breadcrumbs

Melt the butter in a frying pan and sauté the onion. Add the flour and curry powder and cook 1 minute then stir in the milk, salt and cayenne. Bring to boil stirring constantly then add the rice and meat, allow to cool. Shape into croquettes and roll in seasoned flour, dip in the combined egg and water and coat with breadcrumbs. Deep fry until golden brown 2-3 minutes and serve garnished with parsley.
Makes approximately 6-8.

Photograph opposite:
Spaghetti Marinara with Spaghetti and Meat Sauce and Side Salad (Recipe page 258)

Photograph below:
Tacos with Chilli Beef (Recipe this page)

Baclava

A very popular sweet pastry from the Middle East

250g (8oz) almonds, finely chopped
250g (8oz) walnuts, finely chopped
4 tablespoons sugar
3 teaspoons mixed spice
500g (1lb) filo pastry
500g (1lb) butter or margarine

The Syrup:

2 cups water
½ cup lemon juice
1 cup sugar
1 cup honey
1 x 5cm (2″) cinnamon stick

Combine almonds and walnuts in a bowl. Add sugar and spice, mixing well. Grease a large baking dish or slab tin and cover the base with 6 sheets of filo pastry, brushing each sheet with melted butter. Sprinkle over quarter of the nut mixture and repeat process with the next 6 sheets of filo pastry. Repeat until all the nut mixture and pastry have been used, finishing with filo pastry. Make diagonal markings with a knife and bake at 210°C (410°F) for 15 minutes, then reduce heat to 180°C (350°F) and bake for a further 15 minutes. Make the syrup by placing the remaining ingredients into a saucepan. Stir until sugar has dissolved and boil until thick and syrupy, strain and cool. Pour over the hot baclava and allow to stand until the syrup has been absorbed. Cut into pieces and serve cold.

Kaurabriethes

These lovely delicacies are the national cookies of Greece, served for Christmas and New Years Day.

250g (8oz) unsalted butter
1 cup icing sugar, sifted
1 egg yolk
1½ tablespoons brandy
3 cups flour
½ teaspoon baking powder
whole cloves
¾ cup icing sugar, sifted

Cream the butter and sugar together, add egg yolk and brandy. Gradually add flour and baking powder. Mix to a smooth dough. Shape teaspoons of mixture into balls and place a clove in the top of each one. Bake on greased baking sheets at 180°C (350°F) for 20 minutes. While still warm, roll in icing sugar and sift any remaining icing sugar over the top.
Makes 15-20.

Cottage Pie

(Photograph this page)
A dish which was often made in the country to use up leftover meats; but now such a tasty dish, it can be made anytime, and always thoroughly enjoyed.

3 tablespoons oil
750g (1½lb) minced steak
2 onions, finely chopped
1 large carrot, finely chopped
½ cup red wine
1 beef stock cube
½ teaspoon mixed herbs
seasoning to taste
2 sticks celery, finely chopped
2 shallots chopped
750g (1½lb) potatoes cooked, drained
30g (1oz) butter or margarine
¼ cup of milk
1 egg

Heat oil in a large saucepan and sauté meat, onions and carrot over a high heat until golden brown. Add wine, crumbled stock cube, mixed herbs, seasoning, celery and shallots and simmer gently for 5 minutes. Spoon into greased ovenproof casserole. Mash potatoes with butter and milk and spoon onto meat. Brush with lightly beaten egg and bake at 200°C (400°F) for 30 minutes.
Serves 4-6.

Curried Chicken Wings

(Photograph page 293)
750g (1½lb) chicken wings
1 tablespoon flour
1 tablespoon mild curry powder
little butter, oil or ghee
1 onion, roughly chopped
1 cup chicken stock
seasoning to taste
250g (8oz) potatoes, cubed
3 large carrots, sliced
papadams, and sliced lemon for garnish

Toss chicken wings in the combined flour and curry powder. Melt butter in a large saucepan and brown the wings with the onions. Add the stock, seasoning, potatoes and carrots, bring to the boil, reduce heat and simmer for approximately 45 minutes or until the potatoes are tender and the chicken wings are cooked. Serve with papadams, sliced lemon and any other curry accompaniments.
Serves 4.

Photograph below:
Cottage Pie (Recipe this page)

Lasagne

One of the most popular of all the pasta dishes, and because the precooked noodles are now readily available, it makes preparation time so much simpler.

The Meat Sauce:

3 tablespoons oil
1 onion, finely chopped
125g (4oz) bacon, diced
250g (8oz) minced steak
¾ cup red wine
2 x 425g (13oz) cans* tomatoes, roughly chopped
⅓ cup tomato paste, diluted in 1 cup water
½ teaspoon basil
½ teaspoon oregano
1 tablespoon sugar
seasoning to taste

The White Sauce:

2 tablespoons butter or margarine
2 tablespoons flour
2⅓ cups milk
pinch nutmeg
seasoning to taste
extra butter
1 cup water
1 x 200g (16oz) lasagne noodles
250g (8oz) Mozzarella cheese, thinly sliced
½ cup grated Parmesan cheese

*Nearest equivalent can size.

Prepare the meat sauce by heating the oil in a frying pan and sauteeing the onion until tender. Add the bacon and minced steak, and continue cooking until browned, then pour in the wine, tomatoes and tomato paste mixture. Bring to the boil, and add the remaining ingredients, reduce heat and simmer for approximately 1 hour. Meanwhile make the white sauce in the usual way with the butter, flour and milk, add the nutmeg and season to taste, remove from heat and set aside. Grease an ovenproof oblong dish, add the water, and a layer of meat sauce. Arrange the lasagne strips slightly overlapping over the mixture. Cover with the meat sauce, white sauce, and Mozzarella cheese, continue layering until all the mixture has been used, ending with a layer of sauce. Sprinkle with Parmesan cheese and bake at 210°C (415°F) for 40-45 minutes. Serve garnished with parsley.
Serves 6-8.

Dolmades

(Photograph this page)
Dolmades — stuffed vine leaves are very popular throughout the Middle East, especially in Greece and Turkey.

The Tomato Sauce:

1 onion chopped
oil/butter for frying
1 x 440g (14oz) can* tomatoes, drained, chopped
2 teaspoons brown sugar
1 tablespoon lemon thyme
1 tablespoon tomato paste
3 tablespoons red wine
chopped parsley

Vine leaves:

12 vine leaves
oil
2 cups cooked brown rice
1 tablespoon chopped fresh herbs
1 teaspoon grated nutmeg
seasoning to taste
2 tomatoes, chopped
1 tablespoon chopped parsley
2 shallots, finely chopped

*Nearest equivalent can size.

Prepare the tomato sauce by sauteeing the onion in a little oil and butter until golden brown, add the remaining ingredients and simmer on a low heat for approximately 20 minutes, stirring occasionally.

Prepare the vine leaves by pouring some boiling water over them and leaving for a few minutes until softened. Drain thoroughly, and brush each one with a little oil, and place in a single layer on a chopping board. Combine the remaining ingredients and divide equally between the vine leaves. Fold into neat parcels and carefully transfer to the saucepan of tomato sauce, simmer on a low heat for 30 minutes. Serve on a bed of additional brown rice with some of the tomato sauce spooned over the top.
Serves 4.

Zabaglione

A rather delightful light fluffy dessert, and a speciality of most Italian restaurants.

3 egg yolks
¼ cup caster sugar
½ cup Marsala

Beat egg yolks and caster sugar in the top of a double saucepan, until thick and creamy. Stir in Marsala and continue beating until mixture thickens, 8-10 minutes approximately. Serve warm with sponge fingers and strawberries.
Serves 4.

Crêpes Suzette

(Photograph page 292)

This beautiful dessert from France, always looks so intricate to prepare, therefore is usually only eaten in French restaurants. Try them at home for yourself, they really are quite simple to make.

The Crêpe Batter:

1 cup flour
1 egg
1 egg yolk
1 cup milk
2 tablespoons orange liqueur

The Sauce:

125g (4oz) butter, softened
⅓ cup icing sugar
1 tablespoon grated lemon rind
grated rind and juice 1 orange
6 tablespoons orange liqueur
1 orange, peeled, thinly sliced
4 tablespoons Cognac

Make the batter by sifting the flour into a large bowl, make a well in the centre and add the egg and yolk. Gradually whisk in the milk and liqueur to make a smooth batter. Cover and refrigerate for 1 hour. Make crêpes in the usual way, using a 15cm (6″) crêpe pan. Stack the crêpes and keep warm. Make the sauce by creaming the butter and icing sugar together until light and fluffy. Beat in lemon and orange rind, orange juice, 4 tablespoons of the liqueur and melt in a large frying pan. Simmer for 5 minutes. Dip each crêpe in the hot butter mixture and fold into quarters. Add the sliced orange and sprinkle with a little extra icing sugar. Combine remaining liqueur with the Cognac in a small pan or ladle, heat, ignite and pour over the crêpes. Serve as soon as flames subside.
Serves 4.

Chinese Fried Ice Cream

From the Cantonese provence of China a dessert traditionally served with caramel sauce.

3 cups cake crumbs
2 tablespoons Tia Maria or suitable liqueur
6 scoops ice cream
¼ cup cornflour
1 egg, beaten
2 tablespoons milk
½ cup breadcrumbs
oil for frying

Combine cake crumbs and Tia Maria. Roll each scoop of ice cream in cake crumbs. Re-freeze until firm. Roll in cornflour. Dip in egg and milk mixture, then toss in breadcrumbs and deep fry until golden brown.
Serves 4-6.

Italian Cheese and Almond Pudding

1 tablespoon butter or margarine
1 tablespoon dry white breadcrumbs
2 tablespoons rum
1 tablespoon sultanas or seedless raisins
2 tablespoons mixed peel
500g (1lb) Ricotta cheese
4 eggs
¾ cup ground almonds
½ cup slivered almonds
pinch cinnamon
1 tablespoon grated lemon rind
1 tablespoon sugar

Grease a large square ovenproof dish and sprinkle with breadcrumbs. Pour rum over fruit and leave for 10 minutes. Sieve cheese and beat into the eggs. Stir in fruit, almonds, cinnamon, lemon rind and sugar. Spoon into the dish and bake at 180°C (350°F) for 45 minutes or until the top has lightly browned. Allow to cool, then refrigerate, cut into squares and serve with cream.
Serves 6-8.

Photograph opposite:
Crepês Suzette (with Strawberries)
(Recipe this page)

Photograph below:
Curried Chicken Wings
(Recipe page 290)

Dutch Cherry Cheesecake

The Biscuit Crust:
250g (8oz) sweet biscuits, crushed
125g (4oz) butter, melted

The Filling:
500g (1lb) cream cheese
½ cup caster sugar
2 teaspoons gelatine
1 x 425g (13oz) can* dark cherries, drained, syrup reserved
3 tablespoons Cherry Advokat
1¼ cups cream, whipped
*Nearest equivalent can size.

Prepare the crust by combining the biscuit crumbs with the butter and pressing into the base and sides of a 20cm (8") spring form tin. Refrigerate until firm. Soften the cheese and gradually beat in the sugar. Melt the gelatine in ½ cup of the reserved cherry syrup and fold into the cheese, together with the liqueur and the cherries. Pour into the prepared tin. Refrigerate for at least 8 hours, preferably overnight. Serve decorated with cream.
Serves 6-8.

Almond Cake

A traditional Austrian cake.

185g (6oz) butter or margarine
1 cup caster sugar
4 eggs
2 cups flour
3 teaspoons baking powder
1 teaspoon salt
½ cup milk
1 teaspoon vanilla essence
⅓ cup slivered almonds
½ cup grated chocolate

Cream butter and sugar together until light and fluffy. Add eggs one at a time, beating well after each addition, then fold in the sifted dry ingredients, alternately with the milk and vanilla. Arrange almonds over the base of a greased and floured 20cm (8") ring tin. Place ⅓ of the cake mixture over almonds and sprinkle with half of the chocolate. Repeat this process until all the mixture has been used, ending with a layer of cake mixture. Bake at 180°C (350°F) for 1 hour. Cool in tin for 15 minutes before turning out. Serve dusted with icing sugar.

Brioche

A yeast bread, which has a small top-knot. Along with the croissant, the French usually eat them for breakfast.

2 cups flour, sifted
30g (1oz) yeast
¼ cup warm water
extra warm water
½ teaspoon salt
2 teaspoons sugar
3 eggs, beaten
125g (4oz) butter or margarine, softened
egg or milk for glazing

Combine ½ cup flour with the crumbled yeast. Mix to a soft dough with the warm water, lightly knead into a bowl and make a shallow cross on the top with a sharp knife. Leave in a bowl to prove, in a warm place until dough doubles its size. Sift remaining flour into a basin with the salt and sugar. Make a dough with the eggs and then knead on a floured board until it is soft and pliable. Knead the butter and flour mixture into the yeast dough and transfer to an oiled bowl. Cover and set aside to prove, until doubled in size. Knead lightly, break off small pieces and fill greased brioche or muffin tins. Press a hole in the top of each piece of dough and insert another smaller piece so that when cooked, the brioche resembles a "hat". Allow to rise again, then brush with egg or milk and bake at 230°C (450°F) for 20 minutes, approximately. Serve hot.

Photograph opposite:
"The Wonder of Spices", from Param's Indian Restaurant, Woollahra, New South Wales.

Photograph page 296/297:
"Scandanavian Smorgasboard."

Photograph page 298/299:
Colonial Tramcar Restaurant, near the Arts Centre, Melbourne, Victoria.

Photograph page 300/301:
Australia Day, January 26, 1788 remembered. The Rocks Area, Sydney, New South Wales.

Photograph opposite:
Jolly Miller Tavern, Launceston, Tasmania.

Australian Hospitality

The temperate Australian climate lends itself easily to entertaining which is often done on the spur of the moment. A few friends may call in for a drink, a barbeque, the pool lends itself to lunch, or you may want to invite that special person to a dinner party. Whatever the occasion, Australians love to entertain and it doesn't always have to be a formal affair with the best crockery, silver and a special menu. In fact, people seem to prefer the easy, carefree, spontaneous entertaining.

The Australian lifestyle allows us to relax and enjoy our parties just as much as we trust our guests are enjoying them. This gives us the benefit of mixing with someone different, to listen to other people's attitudes, to hear of different lifestyles to our own, to mix around, to listen and learn and offer friendship and hospitality.

Although the barbeque is probably the most popular and casual way of entertaining friends, brunch is becoming a delightful, relaxed and unsophisticated occasion with the minimum of last minute cooking for the host or hostess.

In this particular section, we have kept the recipes very informal, easy to prepare and serve, which will give you plenty of time to mingle with your friends.

Photograph opposite:
"Throw another shrimp on the barbie", a great
Aussie tradition, outdoor entertainment.

Nutty Cheese Balls

125g (4oz) Cheddar cheese, grated
1 cooking apple, grated
½ cup chopped cashews
2 tablespoons chopped parsley
500g (1lb) green beans, sliced
1 head broccoli cut into small florets
1 large red capsicum seeded,
thinly sliced
Roll in parsley and refrigerate.
3-4 shallots, finely chopped
French dressing

Combine cheese, apple and cashews
in a bowl.
Mould into 20 walnut sized balls.
Cook the beans and broccoli in
boiling salted water until tender
but crisp.
Drain and transfer to a serving bowl.
Add the capsicum and shallots.
Toss in French dressing and serve
with the nutty cheese balls.
Makes approximately 20 balls.

Barbeque Dip

250g (8oz) packet cream cheese,
cubed
½ small red capsicum, seeded, cubed
¼ cup parsley
1 large gherkin, halved
3 stuffed olives
1 shallot, chopped
1 tablespoon barbeque sauce
Seasoning to taste.

Combine all the ingredients in a food
processor and blend until well
combined. Refrigerate, then serve
with savoury biscuits.
Makes approximately 1½ cups.

Avocado Dip

1 large avocado, peeled
½ small onion
3 teaspoons lime or lemon juice
¼ teaspoon chilli powder
Seasoning to taste.

Combine all the ingredients in a food
processor and blend until smooth.
Serve with corn chips or carrot
straws.
Makes approximately 1½ cups.

*Photograph below:
Doyles Seafood Restaurant,
Watsons Bay, New South Wales*

Pumpkin Potage

2kg (4lb) pumpkin, peeled
2 onions, peeled
2 apples, cored
2 cups chicken stock
1 teaspoon nutmeg
1 teaspoon salt
2 cups water
2½ cups milk
freshly ground pepper to taste
½ cup light sour cream
chopped chives

Roughly chop pumpkin, onions and apples. Place in a heavy based saucepan. Add stock, nutmeg and salt. Bring to the boil. Cover and simmer 35-40 minutes till pumpkin is tender. Purèe in a food processor or rub through a sieve. Return to pan and stir in the milk. Adjust seasonings, serve garnished with sour cream and chopped chives. Serves 6.

Cheese and Cucumber Passrounds

3 large green cucumbers, halved lengthwise, peeled, seeded
salt
155g (5oz) cream cheese, softened
¼ cup cream
2 teaspoons chopped dill
2 tablespoons pernod
1 teaspoon green peppercorns crushed

Sprinkle the cut side of the cucumber with salt and turn upside down to drain on kitchen towelling. Beat the cream cheese and cream together, add the dill, pernod and peppercorns. Combine well.
Pipe the cheese along the hollowed-out centre of each cucumber half. Refrigerate, slice and serve.
Makes approximately 24

Smoked Salmon Dip

1 x 100g (3oz) can smoked salmon spread
125g (4oz) cream cheese, cubed
¼ cup chopped chives
2 teaspoons lemon juice
seasoning to taste.
Makes approximately 1 cup.
*nearest equivalent can size.

Combine all ingredients in a food processor and blend until smooth. Refrigerate until ready to serve.

Bacon and Veal Pate

(Photograph page 310/311)
6 large rashers bacon
500g (1lb) minced veal
1 onion chopped
2 hard-boiled eggs
1 egg
¼ teaspoon nutmeg
2 bay leaves
Seasoning to taste.

Line a 22cm (8½") x 12cm (5") loaf tin or terrine dish with 3 of the bacon rashers. Cut the remaining bacon and place in a food processor with the remaining ingredients with the exception of the bay leaf. Press into the prepared dish, decorate with bay leaf and cover with foil. Stand in a water bath and bake at 180°C (350°F) for 1-1½ hours or until cooked. Allow to cool, refrigerate overnight and serve with salad. Serves 10-12.

Photograph below:
Ayres House — Adelaide
South Australia

Prawn and Avocado Passrounds

A creamy tasty mixture which is very simple to make.

125g (4oz) cooked prawns, shelled, de-veined, finely chopped
1 large avocado, peeled, stoned, finely chopped
¼ cup chopped shallots
½ teaspoon vinegar
½ teaspoon Worcestershire sauce
½ cup Baileys Irish Cream
½ cup sour cream
½ cup freshly grated coconut
1 teaspoon salt

Combine all the ingredients together in a bowl. Refrigerate and serve spooned onto water biscuits. Makes approximately 15-20.

Apricot Passrounds

A very colourful passround, the filling can be made well ahead of time and chilled until required.

12-15 fresh apricots
250g (8oz) cottage cheese
¼ cup chopped shallots
2 tablespoons apricot brandy
1 hard-boiled egg
1 teaspoon salt
1 teaspoon Tabasco sauce
1 teaspoon chopped chives

Halve and stone the apricots; and place on a flat tray. Combine all the other ingredients and spoon some of the cheese mixture into each apricot half. Refrigerate until ready to serve. Makes 24-30.

Photograph opposite page:
The Waterfront Seafood Restaurant the Rocks area, Circular Quay, Sydney, New South Wales.

Cheesy Spinach Quiches

(Photograph page 310/311)
3 sheets ready rolled puff pastry
125g (4oz) tasty cheese, coarsely grated
2 spinach leaves, shredded
½ small onion, finely chopped
1 egg
3 tablespoons cream
1 tablespoon finely chopped parsley
1 tablespoon French mustard
Seasoning to taste.

Cut pastry into 6cm (2½") rounds, with a pastry cutter and press into shallow patty tins. Combine all the remaining ingredients and divide equally between the pastry cases. Bake at 200°C (400°F) for approximately 20 minutes or until cooked. Serve immediately.

Savoury Eggs

6 hard-boiled eggs
1 small onion
2 tablespoons chutney
30g (1oz) butter or margarine
2 tablespoons mayonnaise
1 teaspoon chilli sauce
seasoning to taste

Remove the yolks from eggs and place into a food processor with the remaining ingredients, mix until well combined.
Spoon or pipe the mixture into the egg halves and garnish with chopped parsley.
Makes twelve.

Pork and Veal Terrine

(Photograph page 310/311)
250g (8oz) minced pork
250g (8oz) minced veal
4 rashers bacon, chopped
125g (4oz) lambs fry, chopped
1 small onion, chopped
1 clove garlic
1egg
¼ teaspoon thyme
3 tablespoons brandy
1 bay leaf
Seasoning to taste.

Combine all the ingredients with the exception of the bay leaf in a food processor, blend until well mixed. Press into a terrine dish or a 22cm (8½") x 12cm (5") loaf tin, smooth top and decorate with a bay leaf. Cover with foil and place into a water bath. Bake at 180°C (350°F) for 1½ hours. Refrigerate and serve with fresh crusty bread.
Serves 6-8.

Photograph pages 310/311 feature:
Pork and Veal Terrine (Recipe page 308)
Bacon and Veal Paté (Recipe page 306)
Cheesy Spinach Quiches (recipe page 308)
Individual Ham and Cheese Quiches
(Recipe page 308)

Stuffed Capsicums

6 large capsicums
2 tablespoons oil
250g (8oz) minced steak
250g (8oz) minced veal
1 onion, chopped
1 tablespoon tomato paste
1 cup water
1 tablespoon chopped dill
¾ cup rice
1 tablespoon chopped parsley

Sauce

1 cup tomato soup
½ teaspoon garlic salt
1 tablespoon sherry

Cut top from the capsicum and remove the seeds. Reserve tops. Heat the oil in a large frying pan, add the meat; and lightly brown, then stir in the onion, tomato paste and water and cook for a further 5 minutes. Add the dill, the rice and parsley and simmer until all the moisture is absorbed. Spoon into the capsicums replace the top, and place in a baking dish. Combine all the ingredients for the sauce and pour over the capsicums. Cover with foil and bake at 180°C (350°F) for approximately 30-40 minutes; or until cooked.
Serves 6.

Photograph opposite page:
La Scala Restaurant
Ballarat, Victoria

Photograph below: Anakie Gemfields
South Western Queensland

Moulded Potato Salad

3 cups potatoes, diced
1 cup cooked peas
1 cup cooked carrots, chopped
2 gherkins, chopped
1 tablespoon chopped mint
1 teaspoon ground black pepper
1 tablespoon gelatine
2 tablespoons creme de menthe
¼ cup warm water
1 cup mayonnaise

Combine the potatoes with the peas, carrots, gherkins, mint and pepper in a bowl and refrigerate.
Dissolve the gelatine in the creme de menthe and the water. Cool and stir into the mayonnaise. Combine with the potatoes and spoon into a wetted 5-6 cup mould, and refrigerate until set. Turn out and serve decorated with sprigs of fresh mint or watercress.
Serves 6-8.

Stuffed Potatoes

6 large pontiac potatoes, cooked
60g (2oz) melted butter or margarine
250g (8oz) cooked prawns de-veined, chopped
60g (2oz) shallots, chopped
1 teaspoon grated lemon rind
½ teaspoon chopped parsley
1 tablespoon chopped dill
Seasoning to taste.

Cut the potatoes in half, scoop out flesh and mash with the butter. Combine with all the other ingredients and spoon back into the potato shell. Bake at 200°C (400°F) until heated through.
Serves 6.

Photograph below:
Martindale Hall at
Mintaro Victoria

Vegetable Casserole

3 capsicums cut into strips
3 eggplants, sliced
6 zucchini, sliced
3 tomatoes, skinned, chopped
⅔ cup olive oil
2 cloves crushed garlic
3 onions, thinly sliced
1 cup chicken stock
Seasoning to taste.

Toss vegetables in oil and transfer to a casserole. Cover and bake at 180°C (350°F) for 1 hour. Serve as entree or as a vegetable accompaniment.
Serves 4-6.

Photograph Pages 314/315
Opera House at night
Sydney, New South Wales

Sausage Rolls

6 slices bread
½ cup hot water
2kg (4lb) sausage meat
1 onion finely chopped
½ teaspoon mixed herbs
750g (24oz) packet ready rolled
puff pastry, thawed
1 egg beaten
Seasoning to taste.

Remove crusts from bread, and soak in a bowl of hot water for 5 minutes then squeeze to remove excess moisture. Combine the bread in a bowl with the sausage meat, onion, herbs and seasoning, place into a piping bag. Cut sheets of pastry in half, and pipe the filling along the edges of the pastry, turning the edge of the pastry over the filling, then turn again so that the filling is completely encased in the pastry. Repeat process with remaining pastry and filling. Score the pastry at 5cm (2″) intervals and brush with beaten egg. Bake at 230°C (450°F) for 20 minutes, then reduce temperature to 180°C (350°F) and bake a further 10-15 minutes. Makes approximately 48.

Barbeque Pork Parcels

2 tablespoons soy sauce
2 tablespoons dry red wine
2 tablespoons honey
1 clove crushed garlic
1 teaspoon five spices
4 pork fillets
2 sheets ready rolled puff pastry
thawed.

Combine the soy sauce, wine, honey, garlic and spices in a bowl, and add the pork marinating for at least 1 hour or cover and refrigerate overnight. Drain the pork fillets, reserving the marinade. In a small saucepan reduce the marinade to half the quantity by boiling gently, then cool. Cut each pastry sheet in half and place each fillet onto the pastry, brushing with the marinade. Moisten the edges of the pastry with milk, and seal. Place on to a lightly greased baking sheet, seam-side down, glaze with milk and bake at 250° (450°F) for 15-20 minutes or until pastry is golden brown.
Serves 4.

Patio Salad

4 x 300g (10oz) cans* kidney
beans, drained
8 hard-boiled eggs, chopped
1 cup finely chopped onion
2 cups chopped cerely
⅓ cup relish, pickles or chutney
2 cups grated Cheddar cheese
2 cups sour cream
*Nearest equivalent can size.

Combine all ingredients in a bowl and serve.
Serves 4-6.

Stuffed Zucchini

(Photograph this page)
6 medium zucchini
30g (1oz) butter or margarine
250g (8oz) minced steak
1 onion roughly chopped
2 tomatoes, roughly chopped
1 stick celery, sliced
Seasoning to taste.

Slice the zucchini in half lengthways and scoop out the seeds and flesh. Melt the butter in a saucepan and saute the meat until lightly browned. Add the remaining ingredients and simmer for 5 minutes. Spoon the mixture into the zucchini and place onto a greased baking sheet.
Bake at 200°C (400°F) for 45 minutes, or until tender.
Serves 6.

Australian Meat Pie

1 onion, chopped
750g (1½lb) minced steak
1½ cups beef stock
½ cup tomato sauce
pinch nutmeg
2 tablespoons flour blended with a
little water
375g (12oz) packet shortcrust pastry,
thawed
1 sheet ready rolled puff pastry,
thawed
Seasoning to taste

Sauté the onion, and meat in a frying pan until browned, draining off any excess fat. Add the beef stock, tomato sauce and seasoning, cover, bring to the boil, then simmer for 15 minutes. Stir in the blended flour, allow the mixture to thicken, then cool. Lightly grease a 23cm (9″) deep pie dish and line with the shortcrust pastry. Spoon in the cold filling, moisten the edges with water and top with the puff pastry, pressing down gently to seal. Trim and score the edges, brush the top with lightly beaten egg and make a slight cut in the centre of the pastry. Bake at 230°C (350°F) for 10 minutes then reduce heat to 180°C (350°F) and bake a further 30 minutes.
Serves 4-6.

Photograph below:
Stuffed Zucchini (Recipe this page)

Ham and Chicken Toss

¾ cup long grain rice
1 clove garlic, crushed
3 tablespoons oil
1 tablespoon tarragon vinegar
pinch mustard
1 tablespoon sultanas
1 large tomato, peeled, chopped
2 tablespoons chopped walnuts
250g (8oz) cooked chicken, chopped
125g (4oz) ham, chopped
1 green capsicum, chopped
Seasoning to taste

Cook rice in boiling salted water
until tender, drain thoroughly. Whisk
garlic, oil, vinegar, seasoning and
mustard together. Pour over hot rice,
stir in the remaining ingredients,
cover and refrigerate until required.
Serves 2-4.

_____

Potatoes in Cider

1 kg (2lb) potatoes, peeled,
thinly sliced
1 kg (2lb) potatoes, peeled,
thinly sliced
1 cup grated Cheddar cheese
60g (2oz) butter or margarine
1 cup cider
1 tablespoon chopped parsley
Seasoning to taste.

Place half the potatoes over the base
of a greased ovenproof dish.
Sprinkle with half the cheese and
season, cover with the remaining
potatoes and cheese dot with butter,
pour over the cider. Bake uncovered
at 190°C (375°F) for 1½ hours. Serve
sprinkled with freshly chopped
parsley.
Serves 4.

_____

Mixed Vegetable and Rice Salad

2 cups rice
3 tablespoons of French dressing
250g (8oz) frozen peas, thawed
¼ cup green capsicum, chopped
¼ cup celery, chopped
1 tablespoon black olives, stoned,
chopped
3 tomatoes, chopped
¼ cup onion, finely chopped
2 radishes, thinly sliced
¼ cup mayonnaise
½ teaspoon salt
lettuce cups

Cook rice in boiling salted water
until just tender, drain and toss in the
French dressing, allow to cool, then
stir in all the remaining ingredients
with the exception of the lettuce.
Refrigerate until required then serve
in lettuce cups.
Serves 6-8.

Mousse of Trout

2 trout
60g (2oz) butter or margarine
½ cup milk
½ cup white wine
pinch of cayenne pepper
1½ teaspoons of port
1 cup of cream, whipped
30g (1oz) ground almonds
cucumber and lettuce for garnish
Seasoning to taste

Simmer trout gently in half the
butter, milk, white wine and
seasonings, until tender. Remove
from liquid and cool. Skin and bone
the trout, and pound the flesh in a
bowl, or place in a food processor
with the remaining softened butter
and the port. Fold in the cream,
almonds. Season, then spoon into
individual moulds and chill. Garnish
with rings of cucumber and lettuce
leaves.
Serves 2.

Photograph below:
Vegetable display, Retail Store,
Adelaide, South Australia.

Malay Style Prawns

500g (1lb) green king prawns, shelled,
de-veined
1 small clove garlic, bruised
½ teaspoon sugar
1 teaspoon cornflour
¼ teaspoon curry powder
¼ teaspoon salt
2 tablespoons saté sauce
1 teaspoon soy sauce
1 tablespoon dry sherry
1 tablespoon peanut oil
2 teaspoons sesame oil
1 large onion, sliced

Marinate prawns in the combined
garlic, sugar, cornflour, curry
powder, salt, saté sauce, soy sauce
and sherry; drain, reserve marinade.
Heat oils in a frying pan and sauté
the onion for 1 minute. Add prawns,
stir fry for 2 minutes. Pour over the
marinade, re-heat and serve on
braised lettuce leaves.
Serves 4.

Tasty Brown Rice Salad

To serve as a hot salad, simply heat all the ingredients together in a saucepan with a little chicken stock, until warmed through.

3 cups cooked brown rice
½ cup corn kernels
½ cup cooked peas
1 cup sliced celery
3 shallots chopped
1 red capsicum de-seeded, chopped
1 carrot chopped
6 rashers bacon, chopped, cooked
¼ cup chopped walnuts
¼ cup mayonnaise
½ red chilli, de-seeded, chopped

Place all the ingredients in a large bowl and combine thoroughly. Chill until required.
Serves 8.

Skewered Seafoods

250g (8oz) scallops
250g (8oz) green king prawns shelled, de-veined
grated rind, juice 1 lemon
juice ½ orange
3 tablespoons orange liqueur

Combine all ingredients in a bowl and marinate overnight. Thread scallops and prawns alternately onto 4 skewers. Grill, basting frequently with the marinade until just cooked. Serve on a bed of thinly sliced oranges and cucumbers.
Serves 4.

Bacon and Scallop Kebabs

8 rashers bacon
500g (1lb) scallops
¼ cup melted butter or margarine
seasoning to taste
little extra butter
½ cup chopped shallots
¼ cup finely chopped parsley

Cut each rasher of bacon into 3 pieces and roll.
Thread the bacon and scallops alternately onto metal or pre-soaked bamboo skewers, brush with melted butter and season. Grill on the barbeque for approximately 4-5 minutes, turning regularly. Melt a little extra butter in a pan, sauté the shallots and parsley and serve poured over the barbecued scallops.
Serves 4.

Photograph Pages 318/319:
Festival Centre over River
Torrens Adelaide, South Australia

Prawn Satay

The Satay Sauce:
¾ cup coconut milk
1 small nob root ginger, chopped
2 cloves garlic crushed
seasoning to taste
2 talespoons soy sauce
1 teaspoon brown sugar
1 teaspoon chilli powder
1 tablespoon lime juice

For Serving
500g (1lb) green king prawns, shelled, de-veined.

Combine all the ingredients for the sauce in a bowl. Place the prawns in the base of a shallow dish, pour over the sauce and allow to marinate for at least 30 minutes. Thread onto metal or pre-soaked bamboo skewers and grill on the barbeque for 2 minutes on each side, basting frequently with the marinade.
DO NOT overcook.
Serves 4.

Seafood Salad

1 x 220g (7oz) can* pink salmon, drained, flaked.
1 x 410g (13oz) can* grapefruit segments, drained.
½ cup chopped celery
1 x 185g (6oz) can* prawns, drained
½ cup chopped parsley
seasoning to taste
½ cup coleslaw dressing
shredded lettuce

*Nearest equivalent can size.

Gently toss together all the ingredients with the exception of the dressing and the lettuce. Chill until ready to serve. Serve on a plate with the dressing spooned over the salad surrounded by shredded lettuce.
Serves 4-6.

Photograph below:
Opal Miners Hut
built of stone and mud,
White Cliffs, New South Wales

Crusty Onioned Lamb

2kg (4lb) leg of lamb
1 egg yolk
3 tablespoons butter or margarine,
melted
1½ cups fresh breadcrumbs
1 tablespoon sesame seeds
¼ teaspoon salt
½ teaspoon mixed herbs
1 small onion, sliced

Remove excess fat from lamb and
brush with a little beaten egg yolk.
Combine butter, breadcrumbs,
sesame seeds and seasonings with
half of the remaining yolk. Press
mixture firmly over lamb. Press the
onion rings firmly into the crumb
surface with the palm of the hand to
form a decorative pattern. Brush
with the remaining yolk. Bake in a
roasting dish at 180°C (350°F) for
approximately 2 hours. When crust is
golden and crisp, cover with foil for
remainder of cooking period.
Serves 6.

Mozzarella Slice

1 x 375g (12oz) packet frozen
puff pastry
125g (4oz) salami, chopped
2 onions, chopped
1 x 310g (10oz) can* 4 bean mix,
drained, liquid reserved
125g (4oz) Mozzarella cheese
coarsely grated
Seasoning to taste

*Nearest equivalent can size.

Roll pastry out thinly on a floured
board. Trim to a 35cm (14") square
reserving pastry scraps. In a small
frying pan sauté salami and onion
together over moderate heat until
tender. Drain on absorbent paper
and cool. Combine salami and onion
with beans, cheese and seasonings.
Scatter evenly over pastry leaving a
2cm (¾") border along one side.
Brush this border with reserved
bean liquid. Carefully roll up pastry
towards border, seal edges. Keeping
join underneath, place onto a lightly
greased baking sheet and glaze
with reserved bean liquid. Using
pastry scraps decorate top with a
lattice design of 1cm (½") wide
pastry strips. Glaze and bake at
200°C (400°F) for 20-25 minutes,
or till pastry is crisp and golden.
Serves 6.

Photograph above:
The Wharf, Noosa Heads Queensland

Lamb Medicis

2 x 200g (7oz) cartons natural yoghurt
¼ cup French mustard
pinch ground allspice
750g (1½lb) lean boneless lamb
Seasoning to taste

Combine 1 carton of yoghurt with
the mustard and seasonings in a
large bowl. Add meat and stir well
until thoroughly coated. Cover and
refrigerate overnight. Thread meat
onto 6 metal skewers and grill for
15-20 minutes. Blend the remaining
carton of yoghurt with left over
marinade in a saucepan and heat
gently. Do not boil. Serve kebabs on
a bed of boiled rice and spoon over
the yoghurt sauce.
Serves 6.

Photograph opposite:
Old Treasury Building, corner of Macquarie
and Bridge Streets Sydney, now part of the
Inter-Continental Hotel.

Fish Mornay

1 cup grated cheese
3 cups cooked, flaked fish
grated cheese, for topping
lemon slices, for garnish

Cheese sauce

6 tablespoons butter or margarine
6 tablespoons flour
3¾ cups milk
Seasoning to taste

Make the sauce in the usual way
with butter, flour, seasonings and
milk. Add the cheese and heat
through. Place the fish in a greased
ovenproof casserole, cover with
sauce and top with cheese. Bake at
200°C (400°F) until golden brown, and
serve garnished with lemon slices
and parsley.

Pork Spare Ribs in Black Bean Sauce

1.5kg (3lb) pork spare ribs
3 cloves garlic
1 apple, sliced
1 onion, sliced
¼ cup black beans
2 tablespoons soy sauce
1 tablespoon honey
1 tablespoon sherry
½ cup water
Seasoning to taste

Place the pork ribs into a baking dish and bake at 200°C (400°F) for approximately 30 minutes, draining off any excess fat. Reduce the heat to 180°C (350°F). Combine all the remaining ingredients in a food processor and pour over the meat, cooking for a further 45 minutes, basting occasionally until the meat is cooked.
Serves 4-6.

Oriental Kebabs

¼ cup soy sauce
2 tablespoons oil
2 cloves garlic, crushed
2 tablespoons brown sugar
1 onion finely chopped
1 tablespoon lemon juice
2 teaspoons grated root ginger
1 x 450g (14oz) can* pineapple pieces, drained, juice reserved
dash Tabasco sauce
4 chicken breasts cut into strips

Nearest equivalent can size.

Combine soy sauce with the oil, garlic, sugar, onion, lemon juice, ginger, pineapple juice and Tabasco sauce. Add the chicken and marinate for 2 hours. Thread chicken onto skewers alternately with pineapple. Grill until cooked, basting with the marinade, and serve on a bed of parsley rice.
Serves 4.

Bacon-Wrapped Cutlets

2 onions, sliced
rind 1 lemon
¼ cup parsley
¼ cup mint
2 cups fresh breadcrumbs
6 lamb cutlets
seasoned flour
1 egg beaten
2 tablespoons milk
3 rashers bacon, halved

Combine the onions, lemon rind, parsley, mint and breadcrumbs together in a food processor. Dip the cutlets in the seasoned flour, egg and milk. Coat with the breadcrumb mixture, and wrap in bacon. Place onto individual pieces of foil, wrap into parcels. Place on a baking sheet and bake at 200°C (400°F) for 1 hour, opening foil 10 minutes prior to end of the cooking to allow bacon to crispen.
Serves 4-6.

Photograph above:
Birdsville Hotel, extreme
South West Queensland

Guinea Fowl and Herb Stuffing

(Photograph page 322)
2 guinea fowl
¼ cup chopped parsley
1 teaspoon chopped rosemary
1 teaspoon chopped marjoram
1 teaspoon caraway seeds
¼ cup chopped mushrooms
1 tablespoon grated Cheddar cheese
Seasoning to taste

Split the fowls in half down the
backbone and breast. Combine the
herbs, caraway seeds, cheese,
mushrooms and seasoning together
in a bowl. Lift the skin from the flesh
of the fowls and spread the herb
mixture evenly under the skin. Place
in a roasting dish and bake at 190°C
(370°F) until cooked and browned
and the juices are clear. Serve with
the pan juices or as it is.

Variation

1 cup chicken stock
½ cup grapefruit juice
1 tablespoon chopped chives.

Bring the stock and grapefruit juice
to the boil in a saucepan. Boil until
reduced by half then stir in the
chives. Boil for one more minute,
pour over the guinea fowl,
and serve.
Serves 4.

Stuffed Chicken Legs

(Photograph page 322)
2 cups fresh breadcrumbs
¼ cup finely chopped shallots
¼ teaspoon Tabasco sauce
2 eggs
60g (2oz) butter or margarine, melted
a little milk
18 large chicken legs

Sauce

3 kiwi fruit
1 teaspoon curry powder
1 teaspoon salt

Combine the breadcrumbs, shallots,
Tabasco sauce, eggs and butter, with
a little milk in a bowl. Lift the skin
away from the flesh, right to the end
of the leg. Spoon the seasoning
evenly under the skin of each leg,
pressing the seasoning so that it is
evenly distributed around the flesh.
Bake at 180°C (350°F) until brown;
basting regularly, serve hot, or cold.

Sauce

Puree the kiwi fruit, curry powder
and salt, and serve with the chicken.
Serves 6.

Photograph opposite page:
Guinea Fowl and Herb Stuffing (Recipe
page 323) Stuffed Chicken Legs (Recipe
page 323)

Bordeaux Prawns

125g (4oz) butter or margarine
1 carrot, diced
1 onion, sliced
1 shallot, sliced
3 sprigs parsley
1 bay leaf
¼ teaspoon thyme
36 king prawns
¾ cup brandy
3 teaspoons tomato puree
1½ cups white wine
2 egg yolks
1 tablespoon water
1 teaspoon butter
Seasoning to taste.

Melt half the butter in a saucepan
and cook the vegetables with the
bay leaf and thyme until tender. In
another saucepan melt the
remaining butter and sauté the
prawns until just cooked, pour in
brandy and ignite. When flames
have subsided add tomato puree,
cooked vegetables, seasoning and
white wine. Cover, bring to the boil
and simmer for 15 minutes. Remove
prawns to a serving dish and keep
warm. Reduce sauce slightly then
beat in the egg yolks, water and
butter. Pour over prawns and serve.
Serves 6.

Curacao Fruit Cheese

¾ cup chopped dried apricots
½ cup sultanas
½ cup orange liqueur
250g (8oz) cream cheese, softened
2 tablespoons milk
chopped unblanched almonds
walnuts or poppy seeds

Combine the apricots in a bowl with the sultanas, orange liqueur and soak for at least 3 hours. Beat the cream cheese and milk together until smooth then fold in the fruit and refrigerate until firm. Mould into a ball or flat round, pressing nuts or poppy seeds into the surface, then chill until required.
Serves 10-12.

White Burgundy Cup

juice and rind 2 oranges
juice and rind 2 lemons
1¼ cups water
1 tablespoon honey
¼ cup sugar
2 bottles white burgundy
1 cup brandy
crushed ice

Place the orange and lemon rind in a saucepan together with the water honey and sugar. Simmer for 5 minutes, then strain into a punch bowl. Add the juice from the fruit, the wine, brandy and crushed ice, garnish with slices of orange and lemon, chill until required.
Serves 15-20.

Ginger Meringues

3 egg whites
¾ cup caster sugar
1 cup thickened cream, whipped
3 tablespoons finely chopped ginger

Whisk the egg whites and half the sugar until stiff, then fold in the remaining sugar. Lightly grease a baking sheet and spoon the meringue mix into six heaps, slightly hollowing out the centres. Bake at 110°C-120°C (225°F-250°F) for 2½-3 hours, cool. Combine the whipped cream with half the ginger, and pile into the meringue shells and top with the remaining ginger.
Makes 6.

Cauliflower with Cheese and Shallot Sauce

(Photograph this page)

½ medium cauliflower
90g (3oz) butter or margarine
8 slices wholemeal bread, crumbed
2 tablespoons flour
1 cup milk
seasoning to taste
90g (3oz) tasty cheese, grated
4 shallots chopped

Divide cauliflower into florets, cook in boiling salted water until tender, drain. Melt half the butter in a saucepan and saute the breadcrumbs until browned. Make a white sauce in the usual way with the remaining butter, flour and milk. Season and stir in the cheese and shallots. Arrange cauliflower in an ovenproof dish, spoon over the sauce and sprinkle with the breadcrumbs. Bake uncovered at 180°C (350°F) for 20 minutes or until browned.
Serves 4-6.

Curried Cashews

2 tablespoons oil
2 teaspoons curry powder
2 teaspoons Worcestershire sauce
pinch chilli powder
2 cups cashew nuts

Heat the oil in a frying pan, and add the curry powder, Worcestershire sauce, chilli powder and cashew nuts. Stir well to coat the nuts. Spread on to a foil lined baking sheet, and bake at 150°C (300°F) for 20-25 minutes or until crisp.

Coffee Cream Profiteroles

1 cup water
1 tablespoon caster sugar
pinch salt
30g (1oz) butter or margarine
125g (4oz) flour, sifted
3 eggs
whipped cream
2 tablespoons coffee Marsala
125g (4oz) cooking chocolate, melted

Combine the water, sugar, salt and butter in a saucepan and bring to the boil, remove from the heat and stir in the flour. Return to the heat and beat until a smooth paste forms and the mixture leaves the side of the pan, remove from the heat and cool slightly. Add the eggs 1 at a time, beating well after each addition, refrigerate until cold. Place spoonfuls of mixture onto greased baking sheets spacing well. Bake at 200°C (400°F) for 10 minutes, reduce heat to 180°C (350°F) baking a further 30 minutes. Cool. To the whipped cream add the coffee Marsala, spoon into the meringues, then coat with the melted chocolate.
Makes 20.

Pavlova Romanoff

1 punnet strawberries, hulled
little caster sugar
½ cup fresh orange juice
½ cup port

Filling
4 egg whites
250g (8oz) sugar
½ teaspoon vanilla essence
1 teaspoon vinegar
2 teaspoons cornflour

Combine the strawberries reserve a few for decoration in a bowl, with the caster sugar, orange juice and port, chill for approximately 2 hours. Whisk the egg whites in a bowl with the sugar, vanilla and vinegar until stiff, then fold in the cornflour. Place on to a lightly greased baking sheet, and bake at 120°C (250°F) for 1½ hours without opening the oven. Leave to cool in the oven. Fill the pavlova with the strawberry filling and decorate with the extra strawberries.
Serves 8.

Photograph below:
Broken Hill Railway Station
Western New South Wales.

Rum Trifle

2 egg yolks
2 tablespoons sugar
1 cup scalded milk
½ cup rum
1 sponge sandwich cake
raspberry jam
2 bananas, sliced
⅓ cup coarsely chopped cashew nuts
1 cup thickened cream
cherries, angelica for decoration

Make a soft custard by placing the egg yolks, sugar and milk in a double saucepan. Heat, stirring constantly until thickened. Allow to cool, then blend in 1 teaspoon of the rum and chill. Arrange one of the sponge cake layers in a serving dish and spread liberally with raspberry jam, slices of banana and sprinkle liberally with cashews. Pour over some of the rum, and top with the chilled custard, repeat with remaining sponge jam and rum. Top with whipped cream, and decorate with cherries and angelica.
Chill thoroughly before serving.
Serves 6-8.

Strawberry and Banana Roll

(Photograph page 326)

1 punnet strawberries, hulled, sliced
3 bananas, sliced
2 tablespoons caster sugar
3 tablespoons Cointreau
3 cups milk
vanilla essence
90g (3oz) butter or margarine
¾ cup flour
4 eggs, separated

Place the strawberries and bananas in a glass bowl, sprinkle with sugar, cover and soak with the liqueur. Heat the milk, and vanilla in a saucepan. In another suacepan, melt the butter, add the flour and stir to a paste. Remove from the heat and stir in the heated milk slowly mixing to a smooth paste. Return to the heat and cook 4-5 minutes, cool. Grease and line a swiss roll tin and sprinkle with caster sugar. Whisk the egg whites until stiff and beat the egg yolks separately. Add the egg yolks to the sauce mixture, then fold in the stiffly beaten egg whites. Pour into the prepared tin and bake at 180°C (350°F) until lightly browned.
Turn onto a piece of greaseproof paper lightly coated with sugar. Strain the fruits and place them onto sponge. Carefully roll into Swiss roll. Serve with whipped cream and extra strawberries and bananas if wished.
Serves 6-8

Cheesy Prunes

125g (4oz) blue vein cheese
90g (3oz) cream cheese
2 tablespoons chopped parsley
2 tablespoons French mustard
½ cup finely chopped toasted almonds
24 dessert prunes, de-seeded

Combine all the ingredients in a bowl with the exception of the prunes. Place the mixture into a piping bag and pipe along the centre of each prune. Chill until required and serve.
Makes 24.

Photograph page 328/329:
"The Night Lights of Melbourne"
looking over the Cultural
Centre, Victoria.

Photograph opposite:
(Recipes this page)
Rear left: Chilled Pawpaw Soufflé
Rear right: Strawberry and Banana Roll

Photograph pages 330/331:
Major tourist motel, The Penny Royal,
Hobart, Tasmania.

Chilled Pawpaw Soufflé

(Photograph page 326)

500g (1lb) peeled seeded pawpaw
¼ cup Kirsch liqueur
4 egg whites
60g (2oz) caster sugar
1⅓ cups cream

For Decoration

kiwi fruit and mandarin segments.

Puree the pawpaw in a blender or a food processor with the liqueur, chill.
Whip the egg whites until stiff, gradually adding the caster sugar. Chill, then whip the cream until a thick consistency is obtained. Combine all the ingredients and serve in a glass bowl and decorate with the fruit.
Serves 6.

Double Layer Truffles

1½ cups ground walnuts
1½ cups sifted icing sugar
2 tablespoons rum
200g (6oz) light cooking chocolate
60g (2oz) butter or margarine
¾ cup condensed milk

Combine the walnuts, icing sugar and rum in a bowl, and press over the base of a greased and foil lined 20cm (8") square tin.
Combine the chocolate and butter in a double saucepan, add the milk, and cook for 5 minutes. Pour over nut mixture, and refrigerate overnight.
Cut into desired squares.

Photograph below:
Opal Mine, Lightning Ridge, famous for
Black Opal, North Western New South
Wales

INDEX